UNFAIR ARGUMENTS WITH EXISTENCE

PS

LAWRENCE FERLINGHETTI

A NEW DIRECTIONS PAPERBOOK

UNFAIR
ARGUMENTS
WITH

EXISTENCE

126168

CONTENTS

NOTES ON THE PLAYS

These rough drafts of plays for a new theatre, or for one that barely exists, these beat-up little dramas taken from Real Life, these unfair arguments with existence (groping toward some tentative mystique) were written in little over a year, dreaming in the back of the Caffè Trieste San Francisco or elsewhere nowhere near a stage. Yet they seem to me very theatrical, in the best & worst sense. People tell me they are "weird" or have "terror" in them. One said there is a "lack of hope." Which I say isn't so, and point to the symbolism of light in several plots. It is for audiences and directors to decide whether these Arguments are "unfair" to life or to those who argue with it, to some God or to the actors. We all act out strange scenarios in photo clothing.

These plays are variations on similar themes, moving progressively from the representational toward a purely non-objective theatre—with still a long way to go. A later book, *Routines,* goes further and faster in that direction. And there is life, there is light, in spite of all. And the light grows: As in *Three Thousand Red Ants*—a little parable of the crack in anybody's egg or universe, through the looking glass—ontology at its most simple-minded.

The Alligation can be taken literally in several ways, depending upon the identity of Shooky. He may also be "represented" as a Man in a Union Suit; his skin may change color; his suit may be striped. Directors should follow their Sisyphitic Noses. Uphill. On the other side of the Indian Head we have grown alligators roaming the sewers of New York. (First performance: San Francisco Poetry Festival, June, 1962, with Erica Speyer as Ladybird, Tom Rosqui as Blind Indian, Bill Raymond as Shooky, directed by Lee Breuer. Second production: Nov.-Dec. 1962, at the Hamlet, Houston, Texas; Ned Bobkoff, director.)

The Victims of Amnesia came into being this way: Two passages in Breton's *Nadja* one night seemed to be spinning in my head, years after I'd read them. The first: "She enjoyed imagining herself a butterfly whose body consisted of a Mazda (Nadja) bulb toward which rose a charmed snake (and now I am invariably disturbed when I pass the luminous Mazda sign on the main boulevards). . . ." The second: ". . . a man comes into a hotel one day and asks to rent a room. He is shown up to number 35. As he comes down a few minutes later and leaves the key at the desk, he says: 'Excuse me, I have no memory at all. If you please, each time I come in, I'll tell you my name: Monsieur Delouit. And each time you'll tell me the number of my room.' 'Very well, Monsieur.' Soon afterwards, he returns, and as he passes the desk says: 'Monsieur Delouit.'— 'Number 35, Monsieur.'— 'Thank you.' A minute later, a man extraordinarily upset, his clothes covered with mud, bleeding, his face almost not a face at all, appears at the desk: 'Monsieur Delouit.'— 'What do you mean, Monsieur Delouit? Don't try to put one over on us! Monsieur Delouit has just gone upstairs!'— 'I'm sorry, it's me . . . I've just fallen out of the window. . . .'" (Richard Howard's translation; Grove Press.) From the conjunction of these two arose my *Amnesia,* which is otherwise far removed from *Nadja*.

Motherlode is a curious little calamity, questioning (on the surface) an obvious premise: In order to attain what one wants in this world, in order to live the way one wants to, one must go underground; not to do so, or to be lured out into the open, may be fatal. . . . It may also be seen as a Pure Escape play. The "trick end" leaves the way open to hopeful new gonopoietics. (Note the terrain: a hairy leg. Prospecting for love, we dig flesh.)

A kind of *Kyōgen* ("wild words" in the Nō theatre— a comic interlude between serious plays), *The Customs Collector in Baggy Pants* was originally conceived for the R. G. Davis Mime Troupe in San Francisco. Naturally tougue-tied (on stage only), Davis didn't use my little monolog, though he did use the toilet. And still does. (He will go down in history.) The best performance of this little "drama of purgation" was by Warren Finnerty in New York circa 1965.

For the visualization of certain scenic detail, I would refer directors to the fantastic drawings of Heinrich Kley (Dover Books, 1962). I am also in some debt to the *manifestes du théâtre* of Antonin Artaud (although he never wrote the plays he made manifest, and I wouldn't want to. I don't love his madness.) I would also mention a book of criticism, *Curtains* by Kenneth Tynan, which first turned me on to certain things that were & weren't happening in the modern theatre. And the critical enthusiasm of Ruth Ford, Vincent McHugh & James Laughlin filled many gaps in the euphoria of composition.

Thus, feeling around on the frontiers of theatre, we may yet possibly discover some "seeking action" in life itself. . . .

L.F.

THREE THOUSAND RED ANTS

FAT

MOTH

THREE THOUSAND RED ANTS

A great big bed almost anyplace by the sea. Fat and Moth naked in it.

FAT: (*under covers, eyes closed*) Mmm— (*silence*) Mmm— (*silence*) M— (*silence*) M— (*silence*) Mo— Mo— (*silence*) Moth— (*Sits up.*) Moth? (*Shakes her.*) Moth? (*Lies back.*) Moth! (*silence*) Moth— er? (*Silence. Closes eyes, whispers.*) Moth! (*silence*) M— Mother?

MOTH: Hmmmm— (*Snore. Exhale.*)

FAT: (*Reaches out, picks up huge alarm clock on floor, puts it to ear, shakes it, resets it, sets it down again, as far from bed as possible.*) Might as well— if you're not going to— (*Reaches under bed, pulls out book, settles back with it, opens, closes, looks at spine, opens, reads.*) "For a long time I used to go to bed early. Sometimes when I put out my candle—" What the—

MOTH: Hmmm?

FAT: You awake? Found your book.

MOTH: Hmmmm?

FAT: (*Fishes under bed, finds new book, settles back, opens.*) Under the heading of— Hey! There's an ant in this book! Stuck in the gutter! One of those cupboard ants you never cleaned out. Caught in the— (*fish-mask of utter despair*) gutter.

MOTH: (*eyes still closed*) You— don't say.

FAT: (*intent on ant*) Ah— freed himself! There he goes. Looks like something's broken. No, there he goes!

MOTH: (*starting up, clutching sheet*) Oooo! (*looking under her*) Where!

FAT: (*intent on ant, mouth open*) He's crossing a "t"! He's— he's— on the word "man"! Still going! With his feelers. He's—

MOTH: (*settling back*) Are you reading that?

FAT: No, a real ant on the page, walking around. Look, there he goes again.

MOTH: He?

FAT: What else! He's crossed the word "man." He's on the word "means." With his feelers. Chop-chop.

MOTH: Chop-chop?

FAT: He's still on "means." Stuck there. Feelers out, every which-way.

MOTH: "Man means—"?

FAT: Uh-oh! (*fish-mask of utter despair*) Down in the gutter again.

MOTH: (*turning away, closing eyes*) Just *like* a man.

FAT: (*still intent on ant*) Means what, means who, means which?

MOTH: Don't ask me! You brought it up.

FAT: (*still intent on ant*) I'm not asking you, I'm asking the ant! I didn't bring it up, the ant brought it up.

MOTH: Brought it up?

FAT: He's made it to the edge, the lower edge. He's—

MOTH: You know how I hate ants and such. Why do you always—

FAT: He's dropping off!

MOTH: Drop dead—

FAT: (*still intent on ant*) Who?

MOTH: You and that ant! (*Turns away, closes eyes.*)

FAT: He's— dropped off. Just fell off. Just went to the edge and fell off— into eternity! (*Searches edge of bed, peers over edge on his side.*) Infinity!

MOTH: (*eyes still closed*) You know how insects frighten me— spiders— or things flying in the room— anything like that.

FAT: (*still searching*) Gone. Disappeared. Imagine that.

MOTH: I have.

FAT: (*still looking*) We'll never see him again. Might as well be dead. (*Cocks an ear over side of bed.*) Ah. I almost hear a crying. Like a tiny wailing! Like someone drowning. (*Searches floor.*) He's down there somewhere. Trackless wastes— bleak— nowheres—

MOTH: Nowheres?

FAT: Wherever he is I'll be thinking of him— crossing trackless wastes— or sinking—

MOTH: Him?

FAT: (*still searching floor*) Like a great desert, or sea— endless expanse— on and on— no horizon. Still a brave new face for each sad new situation—

MOTH: (*eyes open*) What?

FAT: I said "A brave new face for each sad new situation." Feeling with his feelers, confronted with a great, endless, impossible wall maybe, he faces it, faces up to it, feels it— hopeless! The end! (*Settles back.*)

MOTH: He? Or she?

FAT: Either one, as needed. As I said, a brave new face for each sad new situation, a new identity as required. (*Looks over edge again.*) Make up our identities as we go along, on demand, as needed. Improvised names and faces! Improvised characters!

MOTH: Behold the improvised philosopher! (*Turns away, closes eyes.*)

FAT: Exactly. (*Searches floor again.*) Improvisational Philosophy. Exactly. We're all in a gutter.

MOTH: *You're* in the gutter.

FAT: Improvising each step, to balance, counterbalance, to keep our balance— before we drop off, and disappear!

MOTH: I'll disappear too, one of these days, if you go on much longer about those ants you wouldn't let me clean out of the cupboard— (*Opens eyes.*) Why do you always have to live in an old house that attracts ants? Ants eat old houses. That's what they live on!

FAT: (*still looking over side*) New houses eat people!

MOTH: Will you please stop looking for that stupid ant? (*pulling him back*) You know they really frighten me.

FAT: (*Settles back.*) Frighten you?

MOTH: A little flutter. Like when there's a bat or a moth in the room.

FAT: (*looking over edge again*) But I heard a distinct crying—

MOTH: (*Turns away, closes eyes.*) Promise you'll not get up when the alarm goes off?

FAT: Go down crying— disappear! What?

MOTH: Promise you'll not get up when the alarm—

FAT: I dropped it yesterday so maybe it won't go off—

MOTH: In which case—

FAT: In which case we'll sleep through. (*Covers up.*)

MOTH: Through what? (*Opens eyes.*) Why should a retired department store credit manager worry about sleeping through?

FAT: Not retired— fired— I still don't like to sleep through.

MOTH: (Closes eyes.) I always liked to sleep through.

FAT: You always did! So now maybe I'll join you. I did drop the clock.

MOTH: (*Opens eyes.*) You also dropped my egg-cup—

FAT: How can you say it was *your* egg-cup, when we have two egg-cups, both of which are alike?

MOTH: *Had* two egg-cups. Now have one egg-cup. You broke one egg-cup. (*Closes eyes.*)

FAT: (*Sits up.*) Now listen— the calamity of my having dropped my egg-cup seems to weigh more heavily on you than, for instance, those three thousand men in the paper who just got drowned!

MOTH: (*Opens eyes.*) Drowned in the where?

FAT: In the paper— Three thousand troops in Red China that just got drowned in the floods. When the ice broke or something. I read it to you. Also yesterday, like the egg-cup— the two events simultaneous, as it were. Happened at the same instant maybe. And which is the most important to you? The egg-cup! Of course.

MOTH: (*Closes eyes.*) Of course.

FAT: (*Lies back.*) Or— was I dreaming again?

MOTH: (*Opens eyes.*) What?

FAT: (*eyes closed, hand on brow*) What was it? If I could remember—

MOTH: (*Closes eyes.*) What?

FAT: Ah— yes. I was dreaming something like that. (*Sits up.*) I was eating an egg through a hole in the ice. Yes, just a little hole in the roof of the shell— chipped it open with my axe. I was carrying an axe— or my butter knife. A little tap on the side, and off came the top. Yes, just big enough for the spoon, to fish through. Yes— chipped a hole in the ice with my axe and— hmmm— yes— (*Leans back, closes eyes.*) the river yellow and white— underneath— not frozen, underneath— trackless waste— (*Leans over her.*) Hear me?

MOTH: (*Opens eyes.*) You said?

FAT: I said there was snow on the ice, and it broke the ice, and the troops fell through— You could hear their cries as they went under, the paper said—

MOTH: Snow at Christmas! (*Closes eyes.*) Of course—

FAT: Not of course.

MOTH: (*Opens eyes, looking into distance.*) Of course there was still snow— I remember, of course— there was snow still

in the mountains— When we were still living up there, the
year of the big snows— And I cried when—

FAT: When the ice parted, they cried—

MOTH: What?

FAT: What's what?

MOTH: (*turning on him*) Oh, you— I think sometimes you don't
remember anything anymore! Don't you remember anything
in the past anymore?

FAT: Don't remember anything? Quite the contrary! Why I see it
all, just as clearly as if I'd been there myself. I do, indeed.

MOTH: But you *were* there in the mountains, and you don't remember anything anymore— more than a minute— more than
the time something actually takes to happen. All you care
about is the present, still, after all these years. It's as if you
weren't with me at all all those years. As if I weren't with
you—

FAT: "All those years"! It's not so many, really. (*Shrugs.*) So you
like the past and I like the present (*Picks up book.*) and
the future. (*Thumbs through book.*) Now where was I?

MOTH: (*spiteful*) In the future— on "Man means"! (*Turns away,
closes eyes.*)

FAT: The ant was on "means." (*Flips pages.*) Hmm— let's see—
(*Reads, very loud.*) "When he wheeled his penis into the
city square, it went off like a cannon—"

MOTH: The ant?

FAT: Say, what *is* this book? (*Looks at spine, flips pages, reads
again.*) "It is a well-established fact that the world's greatest
collection of erotica reposes in the Vatican. Experts on
sin—" (*Flips pages, closes book, puts it on floor, reaches
under bed, finds second book, opens it.*) What's this?
(*Reads.*) "In the center of the territory of the Assassins
there are delicious walled gardens in which one can find
everything to satisfy the needs of the yearning body and the
caprices of the most exacting sensuality—"

MOTH: Yearning body?

FAT: ". . . Delicious drinks in vessels of gold or crystal are served by voluptuous boys and girls whose dark unfathomable eyes—"

MOTH: (*stretching*) Ah— that's more like it— I always liked "voluptuous boys"—

FAT: "— All is joy, pleasure and enchantment—" (*Looks up, then over at Moth whose back is turned.*) "All is— joy— pleasure— and enchant— ment—" (*Silence. Looks away.*) "All is— (*silence*)

MOTH: (*Turns toward him slowly.*) That's more like it—

FAT: (*Closes book, holds it over edge of bed, drops it slowly, looking into distance.*) What?

MOTH: (*stroking his head*) I said— that's— more like it.

FAT: (*still looking away*) I think I'll— take a bath.

MOTH: Why don't you— (*cuddling up*) take a bath *after?*

FAT: *After?* After the alarm goes off?

MOTH: (*kissing his ear*) Mmmmmm— un-huh—

FAT: (*still looking away*) When taking a bath— (*as if quoting*) one recognizes the true man.

MOTH: (*kissing his neck*) I recognize one— (*kissing his ear*) when I see one.

FAT: (*still looking away*) One? Yesterday in the tub, there was an ant on the edge walking along. Fell into the— ocean.

MOTH: (*Pushes book aside, kisses him.*) Tub!

FAT: (*Gropes under bed, comes up with new book.*) Here's the one I was looking for— (*Opens book, flips pages.*) Now where was I? (*Reads.*) "Like the ant queen, she carries the seed of her long-dead Prince Consort around for years, in a special little sac in her abdomen—"

MOTH: (*turning away*) Ants again!

FAT: (*Reads.*) "There are, in general, only two kinds of ants. There are light-seeking ants and dark-seeking ants—"

MOTH: (*Pulls covers up, closes eyes.*) Ants! Ants! Ants!

FAT: Light-seeking and dark-seeking— (*Looks up, into distance.*)
That reminds me—

MOTH: Of another ant, I suppose?

FAT: Exactly. An earlier ant.

MOTH: (*Opens eyes.*) *Earlier* ant?

FAT: Earlier, exactly. One day there was this ant on the ledger.
The ink wasn't dry. I always used a dip-pen, and the ink
wasn't dry on the edge, and while I wasn't looking this ant
tracks all over it, and I just about get fired, all on account
of an ant!

MOTH: So that was it!

FAT: Well, that was the ant that broke the camel's back.

MOTH: How's that?

FAT: Messed up all my accounting— more or less.

MOTH: Your whole life's accounting!

FAT: I was more interested in the ant anyway. When I was a boy
I remember I always wanted to be a zoologist. (*Looks into
distance.*) Or— was that I— back then?

MOTH: So— a retired department store credit manager dreams
about three thousand red ants in China!

FAT: Not retired. Fired.

MOTH: (*Turns toward him.*) So— there we are.

FAT: Exacto— here we are.

MOTH: Again. (*Snuggles up.*)

FAT: Exacto.

MOTH: (*Kisses him.*) Well?

FAT: Well what?

MOTH: Well, shall we?

FAT: Shall we what?

MOTH: Well, are we (*Kisses him.*) going to— or (*Kisses him.*)
aren't we?

FAT: (*looking into distance*) Mmmmmm—

MOTH: (*Kisses him.*) Don't you want to— anymore?

FAT: (*looking away*) Anymore what?

MOTH: (*also looking away*) If I— I think if I were a deaf-mute and could say only one word a year, I'd save up for two years— (*Laughs.*) and say "Will you?"

FAT: (*Looks in her eyes, kisses her.*) OK—

MOTH: (*turning away*) That's all— just OK?

FAT: After all these years it should be more than OK?

MOTH: (*Kisses him.*) Nevermind— (*Kisses him.*) Better now?

FAT: Better—

MOTH: (*arms around him*) Comfy?

FAT: Comfy?

MOTH: (*rocking him*) Is baby comfy?

FAT: Erk— baby!

MOTH: What?

FAT: I said "erk!" After all these years she calls me "baby."

MOTH: (*Shrugs, turns away.*) After all these years, he says "erk."

FAT: (*Pulls her back to him.*) Nevermind— (*Kisses her.*)

MOTH: Mmmm— hot in here—

FAT: (*Smiles down at her.*) Hot pants.

MOTH: OK— (*Kisses him.*)

FAT: Three thousand red ants in the pants!

MOTH: (*breaking away, disgusted.*) Do they *have* to be red?

FAT: What's the dif? (*Tries to pull her back.*) All— red-blooded creatures— aren't they?

MOTH: (*Throws off his hand. Sarcastic.*) Red-blooded American!

FAT: (*Looks into audience.*) Bloody creatures— All capable of bleeding, that is— even white ants bleed— Aren't there other colors of blood— besides red?

MOTH: (*sarcastic*) Looks like it—

FAT: (*pulling her back*) Don't be— (*Kisses her.*)

MOTH: (*pushing him off, not too far*) Well, I had a dream too. While you were dreaming of your red ants in China, I had a dream too.

FAT: You were the one who was always the dreamer.

MOTH: This time I had a— dream of separation.

FAT: A what?

MOTH: Dream of separation— me from you— I— separated from you— somewhere— a crowd on a hill—

FAT: Where? (*trying to kiss her*)

MOTH: (*holding him off*) Somewhere. (*looking into audience*) Masses of people— masses and masses of people walking, seemingly without aim, soundless, passing by, sadly dressed, a procession. No end to the procession. Only I wasn't among them— you were among them, I think, but I wasn't among them. I was on a high hill somewhere, by myself, looking for you— I think— yes— a lone figure— only I was younger— a few years ago only— a slim girl's figure— like in a travel poster I remember— picture of a great fjord, with water way below— a high bluff above the sea and a girl's figure outlined against blue sky— terribly blue— a young woman in a light dress— you could see through it a little— a summer dress blowing— a light breeze—

FAT: But— (*trying to kiss her*) we're at sea-level.

MOTH: (*lost in her picture*) Yes— a high bluff— distant figure— up there— fragile— summer's day— dress blowing— transparent— scarf blown back— looking down, for something, or someone— as if something had— *dropped off*— the cliff— blew away—

FAT: An ant dropped off—

MOTH: No! (*pushing him away*) A person— (*Turns away.*) *You!*

FAT: (*pulling her back to him*) I'm here— safe at sea-level! (*Brings her head close, looks into her eyes.*) You're as unreadable— as ever— Still, when I look into your eyes I— when I first looked in your eyes, I remember, I thought somehow of— (*Gives embarrassed little laugh.*) seabirds—

MOTH: (*Turning away. Flat voice.*) What's happened— since—

FAT: Nothing. (*Tries to draw her back.*)

MOTH: (*Laughs.*) Fell to sea-level— with his ants!

FAT: (*Shrugs, reaches out, retrieves alarm clock.*) This alarm—
must be broken. (*Winds it, resets it, puts it back on floor
as far from bed as possible.*) I've got to get going now.

(*A door frame is lowered beside the bed.*)

MOTH: (*sarcastic*) You've forgotten. You retired. Remember?

FAT: Fired, not retired! I've someplace to go. (*Indicates door.*)
Someplace important. After all—

MOTH: (*Draws him back to her.*) You have to— (*Kisses him.*)
have a door to go out, don't you? (*Kicks frame of door with
foot. It rises, disappears.*)

FAT: (*watching it disappear*) Now what did you do that for?
(*shrug*) You always do that.

MOTH: (*arms around him*) Don't talk— anymore. (*Strokes his
head.*)

FAT: (*freeing himself, partly*) I may have got fired but I still got
things to do— plenty.

MOTH: (*stroking his head*) What?

FAT: Plenty to do in this world.

MOTH: (*kissing him*) You don't say.

FAT: (*looking down*) Not exactly red-blooded creatures, but still
red and still blooded— bloody—

MOTH: (*snuggling*) Mmmmm?

FAT: They still *feel* cold, don't they, even if they are "cold-
blooded"?

MOTH: Mmmmm (*snuggling*) Who?

FAT: The three thousand—

MOTH: (*very absently*) Where—

FAT: On the ice— in the river!

MOTH: (*eyes closed, snuggling*) S'ppose so—

FAT: The river in winter— ice piled up— couldn't get across—
hungry, probably—

MOTH: (*eyes closed, lips raised*) I've a— (*Kisses him.*) hunger—
(*Kisses him.*) All of a sudden—

FAT: Hunger and cold—

MOTH: (*kissing his chest, eyes closed*) Now— I remember why
    I— married you—

FAT: What?

MOTH: (*husky voice*) I said I've a— hunger too— (*A tall win-
    dowframe is lowered between the bed and the audience.
    She looks elsewhere.*) Yes, a— like a hungry animal, inside
    me— (*short laugh*) When he's sleeping, I don't know he's
    there— but, once awakened, he's fierce—

FAT: (*eyes on windowframe*) Life to be fed, and all that—

MOTH: (*kissing him*) Yes— and all that—

FAT: (*lying back, looking through window*) Ah yes— the sea, the
    sea— whitecaps— such big whitecaps— yes— like a little
    face, each one— hmm— yes— a sea of faces. (*Starts up.*)
    Ah, there's a ship— way out. (*Fishes under foot of bed
    below windowframe, comes up with binoculars, looks through
    them.*) You can see the passengers even. What gay awnings!
    You— can almost see the deck tennis. My, what a good time
    they seem to be having! Take a look? (*Offers binoculars.
    She does not look.*) Beautiful weather for sailing— though
    a little rough maybe. They're coming in, still way out, past
    the reefs— to the channel— yes—

MOTH: (*hand on chin, not looking*) Uh-huh—

FAT: (*eyes to binoculars*) Storm coming up, looks like. Look at
    those breakers— whew— strange how fast the sea changes.
    Just a minute ago, the sea green as grass. Then some clouds
    come over and it's a bed of steel— a plate of steel— all of a
    sudden. (*Offers binoculars without taking eyes off sea.*)

MOTH: (*Not looking, stretches in bed.*) Mmmm? Bed of steel?

FAT: (*Binoculars slip from fingers, fall to floor.*) Damn! (*Retrieves
    them.*) Now I've done it— cracked a glass! Damn, damn,
    damn— (*Puts binoculars to eye, fiddles with focus, polishes
    glass with corner of bedsheet, looks again.*) Look!

MOTH: (*not looking*) Crack, crack!

FAT: Uh-oh! (*Fiddles with focus.*) There— there's something wrong out there. Say— it's— it's on the reefs, by god! (*fish-mask of utter despair*) Look!

MOTH: (*not looking*) Oh?

FAT: Look at those breakers. Gosh— it— it's on the reefs all right. Don't you want to look?

MOTH: (*stretching*) I'm busy. (*Takes out compact, inspects face in tiny mirror.*)

FAT: Gosh— it— it's— she's really in trouble, looks like. They'd better do something, fast. Listing way over—

MOTH: Mm, yes, really in trouble— (*Still inspects face.*) Mmm! Who? (*Raising a little, looks out.*) Not— really— (*Falls back.*) Well, well—

FAT: (*eyes to glasses*) Well, well! All you can say? It's—

MOTH: (*Laughs, sarcastic.*) Striking pretty close to home huh?

FAT: Why, it's going to— it's— actually—

MOTH: (*stretching*) Lots closer than your old ants?

FAT: (*Shouts, waves arm.*) Yes, yes— Hold on! That's it! Don't give up!

MOTH: (*pulling him down*) For heaven's sake! They can't hear you, way out there.

FAT: No— (*still looking out*) Good! Life-jackets. They're lowering lifeboats. (*Raises voice.*) Easy! That's it! Lower away! Lower away, easy! Man those lines!

MOTH: My my, so nautical! Check the block! Splice the binnacle! (*Inspects face in mirror.*) Repair the ravages of—

FAT: Uh-oh, they're in plenty trouble. They've got to get them off— can't get them away—

MOTH: (*pulling him down*) For goodness sake you'd think you were the captain or something! They can't see you *or* hear you. Talking to yourself, as usual.

FAT: (*struggling up again*) But they're going down— (*straining to see again*)

MOTH: They'll be all right. You saw the lifeboats— (*Pulls at him.*)

FAT: Strange— it happened so fast. (*Looks high up in window.*) Ah, there's a plane now— high high up— where the sun is. Can't make out its markings— Red— or Red, White and Blue? Way way up there by itself—

MOTH: (*Starts up.*) Say! (*looking down at bed*) Here's its little shadow— the plane's shadow, crossing the bed— Like an ant! A big black ant— or a little bat— (*Follows it off bed.*) Fell right in here, on us— in our bed even— it's got its nerve— invading our privacy! (*Throws book at it on floor.*)

FAT: (*binoculars still on plane*) But it's— it's secreting something. A bundle or something. Bomb maybe! Oh— no— no. It's a parachute, of course. It's opening! *Two* parachutes.

MOTH: (*looking over side of bed*) Disappeared! And good riddance. It wasn't red either— just black, like any other shadow.

FAT: (*following parachute down*) A real rescue operation— wonderful! They'll save all those people yet. They'll catch those parachutes, with the rubber life-rafts and things— if they're lucky. (*Cranes out window to follow plane.*) It's going on— wiggled its wings! My, how fast it all happened. Must've been God flying by in that plane, just at the right moment! Look at that, will you. Sky clearing now, just like that. Sun come back, from somewhere. And they've got the parachute, by God! Yes— bright sun now— light brighter and brighter, all the time— a real radiance, out there. And the radiance increases— light still growing, everywhere! Yes, and they'll— we— they'll all be saved, after all. All swimming up, clinging— man's indomitable urge to— light— light-seeking—

MOTH: (*shoving window away violently*) Dreamy fool! (*Window rises but can still be seen.*)

FAT: Now see what you've done! (*Strikes her.*) Why you always want to keep us shut in? Always close the window when I open it! Always close the doors! Why, why, why always shut the world out!

MOTH: Oh *hell*— (*voice rising*) I'm "light-seeking" too! But it's— it's not in windows. It's not *out there!* Haven't you (*shaking him*) learned that yet? Imbecile! Ant-head! Prince Consort!

FAT: (*Falls back. Voice comes out small.*) Wh— what?

MOTH: (*Turns away, pulls up covers.*) Oh— skip it! (*very sarcastic*) "Like the ant queen, she carries the seed of her long-dead Prince Consort around for years"!

FAT: (*voice very small*) Say, what's all this about, anyway? What's— what *is* all this?

MOTH: (*closing eyes*) You figure it out!

FAT: M-moth? (*Leans over her. No answer.*) Moth? Moth— I— (*pathetic*) Moth— Is life— a muddle— or a mystery? (*No answer. Looks up at window, raises binoculars to it.*) Empty sky, empty air— (*Lowers binoculars, polishes lenses, raises them to window again.*) Still nothing. Not a cloud, nothing. Inscrutable. Not a sound, not a fucking sound—

MOTH: Not a *fucking* sound, that's rich!

FAT: Silence of the universe, and all that. Empty silence, empty, empty nothing, empty everything—

MOTH: Empty, empty!

FAT: Empty answer to everything!

MOTH: (*opening eyes*) *You* wouldn't see anything!

FAT: *You* won't even look. At least— (*adjusting focus*) At least I *try* to see with what I've got— with whatever equipment— I'm endowed with— with whatever—

MOTH: (*turning away again*) Well endowed, all right, all right! (*Sings to self.*) Oh I can't get it up, can't get it up, can't get it up in the morning!

FAT: (*still looking through window intently*) Nothing, absolutely nothing at all. See nothing, hear nothing— (*adjusting focus without lowering glasses*) Ah— but, now—now there—

there's a— a vein, sort of— in God's eye, sort of— so to speak— (*short laugh*) Kind of a— crack in the ice, sort of— Through which to see— into eternity maybe— as it were— into— the inscrutable, sort of— into the— (*Swings glasses excitedly in all directions, eyes glued to them.*) What a— what a real— what a breakthrough if— a real breakthrough— yes— (*excitedly focusing on audience*) Yes, yes, there it is, there it is, there it still is, by God— no mistaking it— no matter where I look, there's that same little crack, that same little crack—

MOTH: (*from under covers*) Your own! Humpty Dumpty!

(*The alarm begins to ring. First it whispers, then it shouts.*)

THE ALLIGATION

SHOOKY

LADYBIRD

BLIND INDIAN

Alligation: any connexion, situation, relationship, obsession, habit or other hang-up which is almost impossible to break. . . .

Tom Rosqui as Blind Indian in the San Francisco production of *The Alligation*.

(Photograph by Edgar Millhauser)

THE ALLIGATION

Ladybird's house, late afternoon. Very frilly but dishevelled. Drapes or shades drawn. Tall front door, center, an American flag on it. A harp in one corner, a TV set in another, turned on without sound, flickering images visible in the semi-dark.

Shooky is represented as an alligator, at least six feet long, no longer so young. He is first discerned lying in front of the TV, then seen crawling to a window. Raises himself with much effort to sill. Huge head and jaws. Lithe, horny body. Falls to floor, half raises self to window again, falls again, moves to another window, raises self slowly, falls back, half raises self again, falls back, half raises self again, falls back. Lies motionless, raises head, surveys room, windows, audience. Slides over to divan, wriggles up on it, raises head to window, turns head toward front door, quickly slithers to floor. Phone begins to ring, very slowly. Stops as door creaks open.

LADYBIRD: (*Backs through door, shaking umbrella, closes door, puts down umbrella. Rich Mississippi accent.*) My, these Spring rains! Traffic just frightful downtown! (*Turns toward Shooky.*) Was that the phone, baby? Why, I'm soaked— (*Takes off raincoat, hat.*) Soaked right through! (*Turns on lights, turns off TV, kicks off shoes.*) There, now! There we are. Mummy's back again! Is baby hungry? (*Shooky lies with head on floor, watching her. Eyes that never close.*) Didn't I tell baby— (*Inspects divan.*) Baby's been on the divan again! I can tell. Hasn't Mummy told baby time and again not to— (*Shooky turns head away.*) Bad baby, acting just like you were— (*Shooky turns head further away.*) Oh, Shookeee— (*Laughing, she sinks beside him, cuddles his head.*) My little pet! Mummy didn't mean it at all at all! (*Phone begins to ring again, very slowly.*) My own little— Now who— just who on earth (*rising*) could that— (*Picks up receiver. Loud click. Dial tone.*) Hell-O-oh? (*voice rising and falling*) Hell-ooo? (*Looks at receiver, hangs up, turns back to Shooky.*) Now who could— That been going on all day, baby? (*Throws cushion on floor next to Shooky, lies down with head propped up on it, takes out compact, looks in little mirror. Absently. Faraway voice.*) My, how leathery my skin's gotten— lately— (*Closes compact, stretches.*) Aaah— that's better. (*Strokes Shooky's head.*) Miss me? Did baby miss me? (*Shooky lays head in her lap.*) Thought Mummy'd never come back? Doesn't Mummy always come— (*A single knock at the door. Ladybird rises.*) Baby knows Mummy'll always come 'cause baby needs—

(*Ladybird opens door wide. Blind Indian stands full in doorway. Tin cup, glasses, white cane. Ladybird falls back.*)

BLIND INDIAN: How. (*flat expressionless voice, rather pedantic, declaiming*) I Blind Indian. Mine eyes have seen the Glory. (*Rattles cup.*) Blue movies for sale. Help! (*Rattles cup.*)

LADYBIRD: Who?

BLIND INDIAN: (*same tone throughout*) How. Have no doubt Man born in Central Africa. Have no doubt Africa original Garden Eden. No doubt. (*Rattles cup.*)

LADYBIRD: Who do—

BLIND INDIAN: How. Pithecanthropus erectus, he come long way. (*Rattles cup.*) Cross land-bridges (*Rattles cup.*) between continents (*Rattles cup.*) with alligators, camels, horses— (*Rattles cup.*) No doubt.

LADYBIRD: (*Attempts to slam door.*) Why I—

BLIND INDIAN: (*stopping door with cane*) How. Some come over on sail ship called Ark, long before Mayflower. No doubt. Among first settlers here. (*Rattles cup.*)

LADYBIRD: Really! (*slamming door*) Oh, these peddlers! (*Goes to cupboard.*) Really! (*Takes down teapot, cup.*) Really! After all! (*Puts kettle on to heat on alcove stove.*) You'd think— (*Turns back to Shooky, settles beside him.*) You'd think there was a war or something (*stroking him*) wouldn't you, baby? The way they won't leave us alone, wouldn't you, baby? After all I had to do today, you'd think I could have a moment's— (*Kettle begins to sing, very slowly.*) Is that that phone again, for goodness sake? Oh— (*Goes to kettle.*) Well, well, we'll just have a little tea party, just the two of us. (*pouring*) Just like when you were a baby, remember, Shooky? (*Brings full cup, and teapot, sets them on floor next to Shooky, sinks down beside him.*) Remember when Mummy got you at the farm? (*sipping*) You were such a baby, and— and cried like a baby at night— (*sipping*) Too small to remember, of course. (*Phone begins to ring, very slowly.*) You were *so* cute back then! You used to be so frisky, and even— (*phone louder*) Oh! (*Struggles to feet.*) Hell-o-oh? (*Phone click. Dial tone.*) Damn! (*Slams down receiver.*) Well, I'll be— Why, I'll just— (*Sinks behind Shooky again, sips tea.*) Who on earth do you sup— (*Sips tea.*) It's as if— (*Strokes Shooky.*) someone wanted to— (*Shooky wiggles away.*) Poor baby! Is baby all tired out with that old phone ringing like that? (*Tries to pat him. He turns head away.*) Why, I just knew it upset you— I'm going to have to— I'll just have it taken right out, that's what I'll do. I can't have that going on all the time, can I, baby? After all— (*a single knock at the door*) Oh, no, not again. (*Gets up, opens. Blind Indian stands full in doorway. Ladybird falls back.*) Oh, for the— (*Shooky crawls to window, struggles up to look out.*) What do you *want*, for goodness sake?

BLIND INDIAN: How. I come back since I hear two people in room (*Rattles cup.*) but only one speak when I here. (*Rattles cup.*) How come? Maybe second one need help? (*Rattles cup.*) Something funny go on here— (*Rattles cup.*) Need help. No doubt.

LADYBIRD: I'll call the police!

BLIND INDIAN: No doubt. (*Rattles cup.*)

LADYBIRD: (*slamming door*) Land sakes! What was that all about, would you mind telling me? (*Shooky has returned to center of floor. She sinks beside him again.*) I do declare— I don't know what someone's trying— (*stroking Shooky, absently*) Poooor Shooky— you *are* all upset, I can tell, I can always tell, pooor baby. Mummy will fix it— don't worry. Mummy will fix everything. Doesn't Mummy always take care of everything? Didn't Mummy always— (*Shooky puts head in her lap.*) Thaaat's right! Here we are again. Shall Mummy read to baby? That's right. We'll have our little lesson. (*Gets up, takes big Alligator Picture Book from table, sinks beside him again, searches in bag for glasses.*) Now, where in heaven's name did Mummy put her bifocals? Ah, here we are. Mummy'll just read Shooky some from his little book. (*Adjusts glasses.*) There, now. Let's see. (*flipping pages*) Thaaat's right— (*Stroking him with free hand, knits brow, reads.*) "Alligator Mississippiensis— any of several croco-dillians of the genus Alligator, confined to the warmer parts of America, except for one species found in China— (*Shooky wriggles out of her grasp.*) "except for one species found in China"? (*Shooky, having moved to a window, looks back at her.*) "—confined to the *lower* part of America"— Thaaat's right. Shooky! What's the matter? (*Reaches toward him.*) Come back to Mummy? (*Returns to book again, reads again.*) "—except for one species found in China." That's funny. As if anyone ever heard of a— (*Returns to book, knits brow, reads.*) "Like the aardvark, the alligator frequently digs himself an underground retreat"— Underground retreat? (*Phone begins to ring, very slowly.*) Well, I'll be. There we go again. (*Jumps up, rushes to phone, grabs receiver.*) Hello! This *is* the Duval residence. What? To whom do I have the pleasure of— What— what's so funny, please? No. (*voice rising*) No, I have not read "How The Elephant Got His Trunk"! (*very offended*) What's that! Don't— don't you dare talk to me like that! (*Slams receiver down.*) Did you hear that, baby! Of all the— (*Really furious, holding herself in, sinks down beside Shooky.*) Why I— I should have— the very nerve. This man said— first he was laughing— sounded like a lot of people laughing, and then— (*Shooky wriggles out of her grasp.*) Shooky! Doesn't baby love Mummy anymore? Come back to Mummeee. (*Shooky keeps his distance.*) What's— what on earth's the matter, babeee? What's got into you lately anyway? Doesn't Mummy keep all the nasty mens away always? (*Walks on knees over to him, strokes his head. He turns head away.*) Doesn't Mummy always keep them from taking baby away, baby? Aren't they always telling Mummy she has to give you up 'cause you're too big now? (*Puts arm around him.*) Tell Mummy you're not mad really? (*A single knock at the door. Ladybird jumps up, rushes to door, flings it open. Blind Indian stands full in doorway, seems to have grown taller. Shooky crawls toward window, rattles it.*)

BLIND INDIAN: How. I hear call for Help. Small voice cry Help. (*Rattles cup.*) Me very suspicious.

LADYBIRD: Well! You just keep your suspicious nose out of— (*Tries to slam door. He prevents her with cane.*) other people's bus—

BLIND INDIAN: How now? Lady make Indian more suspicious. (*Rattles cup.*) He live Everglade. He have alligator friend. Pale Face come say he want alligator for friend. He say he love alligator. He take alligator. Indian get suspicious. Follow alligator trail. Alligator in jail, on Gator Farm. Need help. (*Rattles cup.*) No doubt.

LADYBIRD: (*still trying to close door*) You— you— you— I'll— Help!

BLIND INDIAN: Me help! (*Shooky rattles window.*) Where help? (*Feels around with cane.*) Where you? You man here need help— How—

LADYBIRD: (*pushing him out*) Don't you dare come in here!

BLIND INDIAN: (*shouting over shoulder as he is propelled out*) Help! I go beat tomtom! I go cigar store call National Association!

LADYBIRD: (*slamming door on him, almost crying*) National Association for the Advancement— and Protection of Alligators, I suppose! (*Sees Shooky at window, looking out.*) Shooky! What *are* you doing in heaven's name? What on earth are you up to— Why you— you're practically standing up! (*Shooky falls to floor. Ladybird sits beside him, taking his head in her hands.*) My iddy biddy baby. Why, you were almost standing on your own two feet, like a big boy, just then. Mummy didn't know baby could— (*Shooky turns away.*) What's the matter, sweetie? Why, you never let on you were learning to do all that behind Mummy's back! (*Reaches out to pet him. He withdraws.*) Oh, you're still mad at Mummy, after all! What's Mummy done to hurt baby's feelings? (*Pulls out hanky, dabs at eyes.*) Oh, sweety-pie— What am I supposed to do? I can't keep you on here for ever and ever and ever, can I now? But— come back— (*He keeps his distance.*) I know— I know Mummy always did say you— you could have your freedom as soon as you were *really* ready— *really* grown up— (*Sidles over to him.*) When you're ready for it, sweetie! But— (*fondling him*) Not quite yet— not— not right away! (*Shooky turns his head away, tries to wiggle free. Phone begins to ring, very slowly.*) Oh let it ring, for mercy's sake. Mummy doesn't care what they say— those awful neighbors! I always said— (*phone louder*) I can honestly say I— always held my head up, at times like this— (*phone louder*) All right! All right! (*Goes to phone very slowly, picks it up very slowly.*) Yes, what is it please? What's that? Please speak more distinctly if you expect me to— Oh, You— vile— (*screaming into receiver*) I want— I want you to know, sir, I don't have to put up with this! I— I— was on this land long, long before you ever— There are ways and means to— No! I am *not* "living with a beast," as you put it! And furthermore, Mr. Citizen's Council or whatever you think you are, I'll live with just exactly whom I want to live with and I'll not— and— what? and I'll not answer to you or any of your— (*Loud laughter at other end. Loud click. Dial tone. Ladybird stands with mouth hanging open, looking at ear of receiver. Sets it down finally. Phone immediately starts ringing again, very slowly, and she snatches it up.*)

ANGRY VOICE: (*very slowly and intensely*) We're— going— to— fix you— lady— We don't like your little— (*Loud laughter on phone. Ladybird hangs up, very slowly, sinks to floor. Terrified expression. Shooky is at window.*)

LADYBIRD: Fix— me? (*biting lip*) I didn't— (*Shooky turns head and looks at her.*) I didn't think it— (*dabbing at eyes*) I thought you were perfectly all right— not like the common

ordinary kind at all, at all! (*Looks over at Shooky.*) My
poor dear! What am I to do with you? (*Shooky turns head
away.*) I— you're at the window again! (*Grabs chain
choker, quickly throws loop of it over Shooky's head.*)
Now— down on your pitty-paws, like a good little—
(*Shooky does not move.*) Please, baby— I'll— I'll make
it up to baby— (*a single knock at the door*) GO AWAY!
(*Knock is repeated. Ladybird flings door open. Blind Indian
stands full in doorway, seems to have grown taller. Shooky
sidles toward door. Ladybird holds him back with choker.*)
Shooky!

BLIND INDIAN: I not Shooky. I come back since I hear two people
in room (*Rattles cup.*) but only one speak when I here.
(*Rattles cup.*) How come. Some funny go on here. Me very
suspicious. Beat tomtom. No one come. How come? (*Rattles
cup.*) Why no one come? Me get more suspicious. (*Feels
around with cane.*) Where man need help? (*Cane comes
upon Shooky on floor near door.*) How! What you down
there? (*Cane feels chain choker, follows it to hand of Ladybird.*) So!

LADYBIRD: (*pushing him out door*) Oh! If you don't leave this
instant, I'll— I'll— (*Slams door on him.*) Whew! What's
going on around here, for heaven's sake! (*Pulls Shooky
back into room with choker.*) What in the— Oh, my—
poor baby's all tuckered out, isn't he? Look at him! (*Strokes
his head.*) And— and all over nothing. It's— it's all so
absurd, isn't it, baby? (*Dabs at eyes.*) Why it's— it's not
as if you were "falsely committed" or anything. (*Strokes
him absently.*)— not mistreated or anything— always
treated like a real grown-up. (*Cuddles his head, laughing.
Shooky shakes her off, turns away.*) Why, Shookeeee—
Doesn't baby want Mummy to pet him with her beautiful
hands anymore? (*Strokes him again.*) With her lily-white
hands— that never washed a— (*Shooky turns away.*)

Oh— (*Ladybird retreats to divan, dabbing at eyes, blowing nose. Sits turned away.*) So— you— want— you really want Mummy to really let you go— Scott free? Forever and ever? (*Dabs at eyes.*) Now that you're— now that you've grown— (*half laughing, half crying*) too large for your britches! (*Blows nose hard.*) After all! After all this time I treated you just like a— a member of— (*Phone begins to ring, very slowly. Ladybird rushes to it, grabs up receiver.*) What is it! (*pause*) Yes! This is Miss Duval herself. That's right. Whom— What institution did you say you— Sounds like the Zoo! Yes, I suppose— yes— you *have* had complaints? No doubt! Well, no, I never considered— You do? Oh yes, of course, I'd be delighted to speak with the Director, if you wish. Who? Mr. Forrest? Not— (*suddenly gracious*) Not Mr. *Hicky* Forrest? Why, of course! Let me speak with him, by all means! Hello? Why, yes, this is Ladybird! Hicky Forrest! Imagine, after all these— I didn't know you were connected— Of course I remember you! No, no, no, I'm not in the big house any more, no— no, it's been some time. Yes— exactly— since Mother left off— What? I said "since Mother left off"— yes— thaaat's right— "passed on"— yes— (*Shooky has gone to window again.*) Hmm? Yes, oh yes, I still do play my old harp. (*laughing, dabbing at eyes*) You remember! Imagine! Except my hands are all— Well, how long it's been! And you've not changed one teenie-weenie bit, I'll— I— I'll wager— I can tell— and— and still a bachelor, I'll warrant, aren't you now? Of course! I knew it, I knew you would be, forever and ever! (*laughing*) What? Oh— (*Looks over at Shooky.*) Well, no doubt about that. How old? Oh about— Oh, I don't rightly know for sure, Hickeee— you never *can* tell their age— (*a single knock at the door*) Well, yes, I *have* had trouble with him, though nothing you'd call— but— I don't see why— No, he's not bad at all, he's never, never a bad boy! (*Looks over at Shooky, waves him down. Shooky does not move.*) He's a real sweety, that's what he is. He's not even— why, he's a real companion, that's what he is, my dear— What? No, no, no trouble with him on that score, ever— really. It's— it's just those awful neighbors cause all the trouble! Thaaat's right. Object to my living with— After all, he's only a boy! As if it was any business of theirs! No, I don't rightly know what their names are. Who? (*a single knock at the door*) No, it's all new people out this way now— (*another knock*) out around here— (*another knock*) Yes— thaaaat's right— dear— (*Shooky rattles window harder.*) I— oh— (*Lady-bird covers mouthpiece.*) Shooky! Get *down*— (*Speaks into phone again.*) What? Thaaaat's right. Shooky's his name. Can you hear him? He's— I— I think he's going to cry! Well, I don't rightly know *what's* got into him lately, the poor dear. Hasn't acted like this since he was a baby. What? It's in the Spring they cry the most? I never heard that before! Well, I— (*a single knock at the door*) if only— (*another knock*) I said if only— (*another knock*) Oh, go away! I'm so sorry, Hicky, someone's at the door who just won't go 'way. Do pardon me, Hicky. It's just some awful blind man— How do I know he's really blind? Why, of course he's bl— I can tell a blind man when I see one! After all— I— You must think I'm— (*Shooky breaks window.*) Oh, my. There goes Shooky again— broke another window! Poor dear, he does so want his freedom— (*Shooky turns head and looks at her.*) And he understands every *word* I say! Baby knows I did promise to turn him loose some day, but— What? Well, if you say so, Hicky. If you really, really think it's for the best. But I never did consider them *mischievous,* Hicky. Baby's got such good manners! What? Oh, I know, I know, I suppose moderation is the— Of course, of course, I know, I know, you just can't change anyone overnight and— well— if you really, really think he'd be better off— if you really— (*Shooky breaks another window, making a strange, inhuman, guttural cry in his throat.*) Gosh, he's done it again! Hicky— what? You're coming— right over? No, please, please, don't do that! No, really I'm all right. I'm perfectly safe! If you'll just hold on for one little moment I'll— Hello? (*Loud click. Dial tone. Ladybird drops receiver, runs to Shooky.*) Well, well, well, well! Shooky! What *are* you up to! (*Pulls him into center of room with choker.*) My little baby— (*Pats his head, pushing it down to floor.*) Little baby's making everybody— (*Sinks beside him, tries to cuddle him.*) Everybody calling up and everything! Just 'cause (*kissing top of his head*) just 'cause Mummy likes living with Shook'ums— (*Phone begins to ring, very slowly. A heavy green light begins to permeate the room.*) Oh, let them ring and ring! We don't care, do we, baby? Baby doesn't care anymore, does he? We don't need all those nasty peoples, do we, baby! (*Sits crosslegged, lifts his head in her arms.*) My poor little— baby doesn't know what's good for him! Doesn't baby want Mummy to tell Hicky-wicky to go away 'cause baby doesn't really *really* want his freedom-dee-dums yet? (*A sudden loud, continuous knocking at the door. Ladybird jumps up.*) Oh! (*going to door but not opening*) Whoever— Who is it please— (*Knocking continues.*) You might as well go 'way, whoever you are! (*Knocking continues. Ladybird shouts.*) You— you'll never, never, never never get us to give up our— give up my— I want you to know— (*Shooky has moved to window again. Struggles up to look out.*) I want you to know you just can't— you can't expect— (*Knocking ceases. Loud laughter outside. Ladybird throws door open.*) Now you just stop that— (*No one there. Ladybird pokes head out.*) Who— who's there— hell-ooo? (*Steps back, closes door. Loud laughter outside. Ladybird flings door open. No one there. It has grown perceptibly darker outside.*) Well now, that's just too— (*Slams door. Loud laughter outside.*) Why, I'll just call the— I won't— I don't have to stand for— (*Laughter continues. Ladybird snatches up umbrella which has been standing partly open by the door. It falls further open as she brandishes it and jerks open door.*) Shoo-shoo! Go a-way! (*No one there. It grows still darker outside. Ladybird sticks head out, raises voice.*) Whoever you are out there— hear me? Whoever you think you are, you— you just get away, hear me? Just keep away, or I'll— whoever you are. Upsetting— (*Voice trails off.*) civilized— people— (*Silence. Ladybird retreats, closes door slowly.*) The nerve! If they think I'm— going to— to change our— Oh, Shookee— I know, I know— you've got to grow— got to change— Everybody's got to grow— We've all got to change— but— but— still— not quite— yet— not right *now*— not right yet! (*Runs to him at window as door creaks open. Blind Indian stands full in doorway, seems to have grown taller. Pushes door wide open with cane.*)

BLIND INDIAN: (*very loud*) HOW!

LADYBIRD: What!

BLIND INDIAN: (*Steps inside.*) You say How? I say How. We say same, only different. How come—

LADYBIRD: (*waving umbrella*) You— you— you— you— you— you— Don't you— dare come in here!

BLIND INDIAN: We say same How. Only not mean same—

LADYBIRD: Just who— you just—

BLIND INDIAN: You say How, you mean How keep alligator pet, How keep alligator baby, How not let grow, How not let free— How keep everything same! How not change, how not see, how not hear small voice—

LADYBIRD: You— you've just got your big nerve busting in here all the time! Just who exactly do you think you are!

BLIND INDIAN: I come back like bad memory, hang round like bad conscience, no go way so easy, hang round neighborhood, always come back— (*Rattles cup.*)

LADYBIRD: (*cuddling Shooky*) Babee, don't listen to nasty old— (*Covers Shooky's eyes with her hands.*) Don't look at nasty old manny— (*The scene grows darker.*) Don't look—

BLIND INDIAN: Me like alligator. We brothers. We see same. I like see free. I no like lady put blinkers on—

LADYBIRD: Don't look—

BLIND INDIAN: (*advancing straight ahead, woodenly*) Look, look! Look see what happen— (*voice rising*) See what happen this country! Who stole country? Pale Face come, Pale Face say "You give up country you get own cigar store." But Indian no like cigar. Indian like peace-pipe. He get cigar. (*Raises middle finger.*) He smoke cigar, he no get peace, he get heap smoke, fire. I no need eyes to see no peace—

LADYBIRD: And— and I don't need my old bifocals to see you're— you're just some cheap— dirty old— Oh! (*Tries to cover Shooky's head.*) Close your little— don't even—

BLIND INDIAN: (*Stands erect over both, feeling them with cane.*) See very clear. All very clear. Heap clear. Heap bad scene.

LADYBIRD: (*Shielding Shooky, screams at Indian.*) You just watch out, now! Hear me? They'll— they're coming. He'll— they'll have you— They'll— we'll—

BLIND INDIAN: You got bifocal, you got split vision, you see alligator bottom half, top half you see real people— (*Bends down, finds chain on Shooky.*) How—

LADYBIRD: Oh! You mean old smelly— (*Tries to pull Shooky away.*)

BLIND INDIAN: (*pulling Shooky toward door*) Step on gas! Shoo— shoo! (*Gets Shooky to door, casts off chain.*) There! You free, man! Scram, so long— (*Urges Shooky with foot.*) Hurry, hurry! (*Shooky does not move.*)

LADYBIRD: Help, help! Someone save our— my—

BLIND INDIAN: (*urging with foot*) Save self! Scram! You free but you no know which way go. You still feel chain, you think you still got chain, you no got chain! (*Shooky begins to move.*)

LADYBIRD: (*throwing herself upon Shooky*) Baby, baby! I thought you didn't really, really— (*Great vines and leaves begin to push in through broken windows.*)

BLIND INDIAN: (*urging with foot*) Go, go, go!

LADYBIRD: (*glaring up at Indian*) They— *they* sent you, didn't they! You horrible— old— (*Vines and leaves begin to fill doorway.*)

BLIND INDIAN: (*Draws self to full height.*) Nobody send! Indian no go-between— (*Bends down. Stage whisper to Shooky.*) Me no go-go between. You go, I go— I go, you follow— Time for Revolution! Go, go! Revolution happen now!

LADYBIRD: (*arms still around Shooky, still holding him back.*) Oh, babeee! Don't leave me! How'll we manage without you! (*kissing Shooky's head*) Oh, sweetie— (*Shooky gives a small roar.*) Oh, Shookee! Shook—

BLIND INDIAN: (*stage whisper in Shooky's ear*) Go, go! Make like free! You free, but watch out Indian Giver— Lord give, Lord take away! Hurry! (*Shooky raises head very slowly, turns head to audience very slowly. Unblinking eyes. Remains in this position. Indian straightens up. Unblinking eyes. Great vines and leaves have completely filled the doorway.*)

LADYBIRD: Oh, oh— (*struggling up*) This is just too much! After all! I'll just run out and— (*Runs against matted vines at door.*) Oh! (*Falls, ripping dress on vines.*) Help! Somebody! I give up! Let me out! (*Half rises, rushes against vines again, further ripping dress.*) Help— please— (*feebly*) Pleeease— (*As scene grows still darker, the walls themselves seem to have become mats of vines.*) Yes— please. I give up— I do, I do— I see now— Yes, I do, I do— It's— it's *not* too late—

BLIND INDIAN: (*Standing erect, hooks Ladybird with crook of cane.*) Where you think you go? You make zoo, you live in zoo. You no get out so easy from own jail you make so easy. You make tepee, you live in tepee. You grow jungle, you live jungle. Jungle Jim take over! (*Bends down suddenly, pulls Ladybird up, shakes her.*) Listen, lady! Listen small voice! Like I say, what happen to country? Noble Redskin drink firewater, Noble Redskin see red, begin see who steal America, begin see what happen America— Sweet Land! America lose Indian Path, America no care, America keep pet alligator, America do snake dance, America smoke big black cigar, America big mad movie! (*Stops shaking Ladybird.*) You— you— (*Drops her gently.*) You— (*Puts hands to eyes very slowly.*)

LADYBIRD: (*falling heavily next to Shooky*) Oh, oh— too late— (*very small voice*) What have I— we— Shookeeee— (*Stretches full length on him, kissing him.*) Shookeeee— too late— too late!

(*Shooky suddenly roars and rolls over on top of Ladybird with a great thrashing. Ladybird makes a strange, inhuman, guttural cry in her throat.*)

BLIND INDIAN: (*hand still over eyes*) Help— (*Rattles cup.*) Help— (*Ladybird cries again.*) Help— (*Scans horizon, beyond audience, hand to brow, Indian fashion.*) Help— (*Waves cane wildly at audience.*) Help! (*very loud*) HELP!

(*Long silence. Ladybird lies still under Shooky. The TV flickers on in the darkness.*)

THE VICTIMS OF AMNESIA

NIGHT CLERK

MARIE

YOUNG WOMAN

GIRL

BABY

[The female parts may or may not all be played by the same person.]

THE VICTIMS OF AMNESIA

SCENE ONE

*A hotel desk. Third class. A sign: STATION HOTEL—
TRANSIENTS. Through transom-like windows above and
behind the desk can be seen innumerable feet ceaselessly
passing on the sidewalk which cuts across the windows.
At right, a short ramp leads down from the street. At
left, a square stairwell with carpeted stairs leading up.*

*The Night Clerk, neither old nor young, glasses, green eye-
shade, sits at desk, reading. Sound of train whistles far off.
Enter Marie, a big beautiful woman in her late thirties.
Elegant maternity dress, a bit shabby.*

MARIE: (*at foot of ramp, uncertainly*) Good— evening— (*coming up to desk*) Good evening!

NIGHT CLERK: (*Looks up over glasses.*) Eh?

MARIE: I'd like a room, if you please.

NIGHT CLERK: (*looking her over*) For what purpose?

MARIE: I beg your pardon?

NIGHT CLERK: I said for what purpose.

MARIE: To what purpose?

NIGHT CLERK: (*very pedantic*) For what purpose do you— uh—
desire a chamber? That is, just what do you propose to—

MARIE: Well! (*naturally exasperated*) Perhaps, my dear man, I don't "desire a chamber" at all. Perhaps I am just one of these— peddlers!

NIGHT CLERK: I can tell.

MARIE: Or panhandlers!

NIGHT CLERK: My dear lady, I have been at this desk for a number of years, and I have developed an acute sense of—

MARIE: Or— or one of your—

NIGHT CLERK: I have developed quite a reputation for—

MARIE: Tramps!

NIGHT CLERK: For— perspicacity in these matters—

MARIE: Or—

NIGHT CLERK: "Maurice" they always say, "Maurice can see them coming!" And that, my dear lady, is why I'm hired to—

MARIE: My dear man—

NIGHT CLERK: I know someone who wants a room when I see one, and you, my dear lady, have that look.

MARIE: My dear man, but everyone has that look—

NIGHT CLERK: Yes, my dear lady, but you have neglected to answer the questions which the Management insists must be answered before one can enter this Establishment.

MARIE: What questions? Now, see here, I've had enough, I'm not in the habit of—

NIGHT CLERK: That's obvious. Seems like all we get is people who're "not in the habit of," or who've "had enough"!

MARIE: My dear man, it just so happens, if you will allow me, it just so happens that I am about to have a baby, so if you will please show me up as quickly as—

NIGHT CLERK: Ah, so? (*Removes glasses to get a better look.*)

MARIE: Ah, so! Are you Chinese or something? I tell you I was just on my way to catch my train, when—

NIGHT CLERK: Caught short, is that it? (*Laughs nastily.*)

MARIE: If you must! Now if you will please—

NIGHT CLERK: (*shoving large open register at her*) If you will please register! (*Returns to his reading; mumbling.*) Caught short! Everybody always "caught short." Why doesn't someone ever arrange—

MARIE: (*After writing a word or two, stops with pen poised.*) Of course— that is— (*Finally drops pen.*)

NIGHT CLERK: What's the trouble now, if you please? Nobody seems able to—

MARIE: It's just that— you see, I have a very, very poor memory. In fact (*short laugh*) I seem to have no memory at all.

NIGHT CLERK: (*bending over register, pointing*) Right here, please. Just fill in "Name"— "Point of Origin"— "Destination"— "Service Number" if any— "Representing"—

MARIE: "Representing"? I'm not "representing"— I'm "expecting"—

NIGHT CLERK: I did not make up the—

MARIE: "Point of Origin"? What does that have to do with—

NIGHT CLERK: Of course. They're quite strict about all that— around here. Especially in this district, if you know what I mean. (*Laughs nastily.*)

MARIE: I do not know what you mean!

NIGHT CLERK: No funny business around here! The Management requires—

MARIE: Of course, of course, I understand all that.

NIGHT CLERK: Well, then? (*Wiggles register.*)

MARIE: Of course, all right— as you say. (*Takes up pen again.*) It's urgent— (*Makes as if to fill in register again, stops, pen poised. Clerk has gone back to his reading.*) It's— it's just that I've no— Well— (*Sneaks a look at Clerk who continues reading.*) I'll just— make up a nice— (*Writes in register, gaily, with a flourish.*) There you are, my man!

NIGHT CLERK: (*without looking*) Thank you, my dear lady! Baggage?

MARIE: No, of course not. I told you I was just going to catch my
little train when—

NIGHT CLERK: Right. That'll be three dollars, then. Transients
must pay in advance, in any case.

MARIE: (*slapping money down on desk*) Then why did you ask
me for baggage, then?

NIGHT CLERK: (*pocketing money*) Thank you! (*Takes a key.*)
This way please, if you please. (*Stops short.*) Ah, one more
thing— If you will not make any undue noises during the
night. Please note the sign you will find in your room: "Quiet
is requested for the benefit of those who have retired."

MARIE: What is this, a Pullman car or something!

NIGHT CLERK: (*Leading the way upstairs, left, pauses proudly.*)
It just so happens, my dear lady, I happen to have been a
conductor once upon a time—

MARIE: If you will please conduct me—

(*They disappear up stairs. In a moment, Clerk returns, sits,
starts to read again, picks nose, takes out watch on chain,
consults it, winds it, returns it to pocket, peers around lobby,
gets up half way, cranes neck to see upstairs, ducks under
desk, comes up with old conductor's cap, adjusts it on head
over green visor, humming martial tune, ducks under desk
again, comes up with old Army rifle, peers upstairs again,
strides out from behind desk, snaps to attention, rifle at
side.*)

NIGHT CLERK: (*performing appropriate motions with gusto*)
Pa-rade, rest!— Ten-chun!— R-i-i-ght shoulder— h-arms!
(*each command a harsh stage whisper, a kind of braying
noise*) Forward— h-arch!— Companeeee— h-halt! Forward— h-harch! (*Hums "Over There" between commands.*)
By the right flank— h-arch! By the right flank— h-harch!
Companeee— h-halt! About— h-ace! Present— h-arms!

(*Stops short, peers upstairs, hears noise, scurries back to desk, stowing hat and gun under it, picks up magazine as Marie descends.*)

MARIE: If you please—

NIGHT CLERK: (*reading*) Mmmm?

MARIE: If you please— I'm going out for a bit of air— It seems I was—

NIGHT CLERK: Mmmmm?

MARIE: It seems I was just (*short laugh*) a bit premature.

NIGHT CLERK: (*still reading*) Pre— mature? Mmm?

MARIE: Yes, Mister Conductor. If you will be so kind— each time I come in will you do me a little favor?

NIGHT CLERK: Mmmmmm?

MARIE: Each time I come in, I'll tell you my name, and each time please tell me the number of my room—

NIGHT CLERK: (*still reading*) Of course. The number of your room, each time.

MARIE: That's right, if you will. You see, it's just that I really have no memory at all.

NIGHT CLERK: Mmmm— of course— just as you say.

MARIE: Good evening, then. (*Goes out, right.*)

NIGHT CLERK: Mmm. No memory at all. Where was I exactly? (*Thumbs magazine, reads, closes register without looking, picks nose, eats it, takes out watch, consults it, returns it to pocket, ducks behind desk, comes up with rifle, quickly replaces it as Marie returns, in a great hurry.*)

MARIE: Mazda!

NIGHT CLERK: What?

MARIE: If you please—(*tapping closed register*) I gave you the name Mazda— Mrs. Mazda—

NIGHT CLERK: (*returning to magazine*) Of course. Room thirty-five.

MARIE: Thank you! (*Starts upstairs.*)

NIGHT CLERK: I never forget a face! (*Hums martial tune.*)

MARIE: (*disappearing upstairs*) Who could!

NIGHT CLERK: (*looking up blankly*) Who could? (*Peers around
    lobby quickly, cranes to see upstairs, ducks under desk,
    pulls out rifle, raises it to eye, humming "Over There," aims
    it upstairs, slowly swings it around until aim is on audience,
    stops humming, lowers rifle slowly until it is aimed at front
    row of audience. The only sound is the sound of passing
    feet.*)

SCENE TWO

(This scene must be played with intensity, in a classic tragic manner, absolutely straight, not in any way to suggest comic overtones. Every attempt must be made to convince the spectators of the literal reality of what is happening, since it does happen & is real.)

Marie's room in the hotel. Sound of train whistles far off. Clock tolls: Two o'clock. A high old bed next to window, left, with drawn shade. Marie upon the bed, in hard labor, panting, sweating, moaning; after very great travail, finally brings forth from under skirt an enormous lighted bulb on extension cord; holds it up; it grows brighter; a crying is heard, growing louder as the light brightens. Marie rolls up window shade, leans out, looks down, dangles bulb out window by cord, lowers it gently to ground, takes out large scissors, cuts cord very carefully, holds end of it a long moment, finally drops it outside, looks down a long moment, hears louder crying, draws shade, lies back exhausted, eyes closed. Darkness.

Sound of train whistles far off. The room lightens. Clock tolls Two. Marie stretches, turns restlessly, sits up, lies back again, hand over eyes, stretches, starts to hum, starts to sing to self, laughs, breaks off, stretches, turns restlessly, hugs huge pillow or bolster, sings to self, breaks off, moans, draws knees up, moans louder; in labor again; after very great travail, finally brings forth medium-size lighted bulb on extension cord; holds it up; a crying is heard. Same business: raising shade, leaning out, dangling bulb out window, cutting cord, dropping it, lying back exhausted, eyes closed, shade drawn again. Darkness.

Sound of train whistles far off. The room lightens. Clock tolls Two. Same business: labor again. Finally brings forth small lighted bulb on extension cord. Same business: raising shade, lowering bulb, cutting cord, drawing shade again, lying back, eyes closed. Darkness.

Clock tolls Two. Sound of train whistles far off.

SCENE THREE

The hotel desk. Night Clerk reads, picks nose, takes out watch as clock tolls Two. Feet outside windows have increased their pace, some running, others halting and turning. Train whistles far off. A buxom young woman, clothes covered with mud, bleeding, out of breath, stumbles down ramp at right, falls to floor, struggles up, approaches desk, an electric extension cord trailing after her.

YOUNG WOMAN: Mazda!

NIGHT CLERK: (*still reading*) Mmmm— what? How's that?

YOUNG WOMAN: I said "Mazda."

NIGHT CLERK: (*closing magazine*) You don't say! (*looking her over*) Well, well! (*Laughs nastily.*) Nice "bulbs" I must say! Miss— (*Laughs nastily.*) Mazda!

YOUNG WOMAN: I'd— I'd like the number of my room, if you please.

NIGHT CLERK: Now, listen here— the "Mazda" lady's already gone upstairs— and (*opening register*) without properly filling in the register, either. (*very pedantic*) Questions which the Management of this Establishment insists—

YOUNG WOMAN: I'm very sorry, but it's me— I'm the "Mazda lady" and I've just fallen from my window. What's my room, if you please?

NIGHT CLERK: Don't try to fool me, young lady! Trying to pull a fast one or something— two for the price of one, is that what you're up to? I just told you, the Mazda lady has already gone to her room, and who the hell— where did you come—

YOUNG WOMAN: I'm very sorry you won't believe me— the *name* is Mazda.

NIGHT CLERK: (*scanning register*) Mazda? Mazda? Mazda what? Who Mazda? Do you realize— have you any idea just how many Mazdas there must be in this world? How am I supposed to keep up with them, you mind telling me, when— (*sputtering*) when they won't even fill in the blanks? I tell you, it's— (*Runs hands through hair.*) I tell you it's like pulling teeth. As if they couldn't even remember— as if nobody could remember exactly where in hell they were from and so forth— questions which the Management requires before— Why just yesterday, a whole band of girl scouts, mind you, comes running in here without their leader. Lost their leader somewhere, can you beat that! Didn't know—

YOUNG WOMAN: Please, all I asked was—

NIGHT CLERK: (*growing more and more excited*) And I'm responsible, do you realize that? I don't suppose such a thing would ever enter your bulb, would it? (*Laughs nastily.*)

YOUNG WOMAN: My what? I merely asked you for—

NIGHT CLERK: I said I'm responsible, I'm the one with the responsibility of obtaining all the proper required information from each and every client— from every last transient who comes through here. (*Shakes head, running hands through hair.*) From every last one, do you hear me!

YOUNG WOMAN: Please, I'm not interested in all—

NIGHT CLERK: All these comings and goings, forever and ever and ever! (*scanning register*) All right! If you will please just fill in these important basic questions—

YOUNG WOMAN: (*Takes pen, holds it dumbly.*) I'm— very sorry—
It's as if some light went out someplace and I can't—

NIGHT CLERK: (*jumping up, voice rising*) Some light went out?
That's rich! The name is Mazda, and she tells me some light
went out! As if— as if— that's any excuse for not— (*sputtering*) for not knowing— for not being able to— give the
most elementary, the most basic inform— (*absolutely disgusted*) Oh, the hell with it!

YOUNG WOMAN: I merely—

NIGHT CLERK: (*raving on*) Always this eternal struggle to find
out the simplest basic facts as to—

YOUNG WOMAN: It's just that I—

NIGHT CLERK: You'd think they'd all be eager to tell you simple
things like that, eager to tell you, but no, not at all, nothing
of the sort, no, it's like—

YOUNG WOMAN: Please, I merely asked for— I can't help it if—

NIGHT CLERK: (*wagging his finger at her*) Let me tell you, young
lady, I'm not just one of these no-good clerks without any
interest in—

YOUNG WOMAN: Please, if you would please, please—

NIGHT CLERK: All my life, young lady, I've had an enquiring mind.
A bright boy, I was, yessir, smart, if you know what I mean.
"Maurice," they used to say—

YOUNG WOMAN: If only you would please just tell me what room—

NIGHT CLERK: "Maurice," they used to say, "Maurice, you'll go a
long way, Maurice—" always asking questions about everything, yes, like when they told me it was the stork and all
that, I'd say "Well, where did *he* come from?" and what
would I get for an answer?

YOUNG WOMAN: Please, what does— can't you see I—

NIGHT CLERK: And what— what kind of answers have I ever
gotten to anything, would you (*voice rising again*) would
you mind telling me, what do I get in the end— nothing?

No real replies to anything! And— and why do I keep holding on to this stupid little asinine pilfering little half-ass—

YOUNG WOMAN: Sir! Please—

NIGHT CLERK: —little job for? Plenty of time to read, they told me! Bah! You'd think a night clerk in an Establishment like this would really be in a position to collect some real dope, some real inside dope on people— their little vital statistics, their little secrets, the little things that don't come out in the daylight, what really makes them tick. But, no! It's the same as any place else, the same as before, nobody telling you nothing! Reading don't tell nothing, and people don't tell nothing! It's as if—

YOUNG WOMAN: But I just told you, the name is Mazda, and all I asked was, plainly and simply, the number of the—

NIGHT CLERK: Mazda, Mazda, Mazda! Well, Mazda's in thirty-five, if you have to know, if it's any business of yours, whoever you—

YOUNG WOMAN: Thank *you!* (*Goes up, left.*)

NIGHT CLERK: OK, OK, OK! I don't give one flying ferk what— (*flipping pages of magazine*) Thirty-five! (*Settles down, picks nose, eats it, takes out watch as clock tolls Two.*)

Train whistles far off. Twelve-year-old girl skips down ramp, right, trips over skip-rope, falls, entangled in cord, disentangles self, looks at cord curiously, throws it away, struggles up, bleeding, clothes torn.

GIRL: Mazda?

NIGHT CLERK: (*still reading*) Mmmm?

GIRL: Mazda— what room is Mazda, please?

NIGHT CLERK: (*fierce scowl*) Ma-ma! (*mimicking her*) Ma-ma!

GIRL: No, sir— Mazda.

NIGHT CLERK: (*holding on to self*) Now, listen here, little girl—

GIRL: Yes, sir?

NIGHT CLERK: Let me just— (*very slowly*) tell you a thing or two or—

GIRL: Yes, sir?

NIGHT CLERK: (*drumming fingers on desk*) When I was in the Service, we did not have to put up with this kind of— ring around the— (*Sputters.*) Blindman's bluff—

GIRL: Yes, sir?

NIGHT CLERK: No, sir, we did not! "Mop-em-up Maurice," I was known as—

GIRL: Yes, sir?

NIGHT CLERK: Now, listen here, my little friend— (*very slowly*) I just want you to pull yourself together and try to calmly—

GIRL: (*very calmly*) Yes, sir?

NIGHT CLERK: —tell me exactly just what this is all about— just what exactly is going on around here? Mmmm?

GIRL: Sir, I just fell and—

NIGHT CLERK: Now, now, listen here, this is getting to be— just too much! Why, last week a whole band of German·tourists just fell like that out of nowhere— with cameras! And wanted to know where— as if I could— as if I were some kind of—

GIRL: Sir?

NIGHT CLERK: (*taking off glasses to inspect her*) Well— you are a polite little one, at least— (*scanning register*) Now, if you will be so kind, my dear little friend—

GIRL: Sir?

NIGHT CLERK: I don't see any registration for a minor by the name of—

GIRL: Mazda. What room is—

NIGHT CLERK: Mazda! Now, listen, you— (*voice beginning to rise again*) You, don't you try to— (*shaking finger, rising*) try to pull that old dodge on me again, hear me? I know exactly how many clients are assigned to each room and I happen to know, I happen to have been on duty when room thirty-five was let, and it's a single, and—

GIRL: Thirty-five? Thank you! (*Runs & skips up, left.*)

NIGHT CLERK: (*Collapses on seat.*) Oh, for Gad's sake! (*absolutely disgusted*) I give up! I'm just not cut out to— I guess I— (*Smooths hair, adjusts visor, picks up magazine, mumbling, flips pages.*) Thirty-five! What a friggin farce! As if— (*Mumble peters out. Picks nose, takes out watch as clock tolls Two. A baby carriage slowly rolls down ramp, right, and comes to stop near desk. Train whistles far off.*)

BABY: (*dishevelled, bleeding, in carriage*) Na-na-na—

NIGHT CLERK: (*jumping up*) Wa-a-i-i-t a minute! Just wait one minute! What— is this, a nursery, for Gad's sake? Orphans' Home or something?

BABY: Na-na-na- na-na-na-

NIGHT CLERK: (*advancing to carriage*) Bah, bah! Now, who dropped *you* down the chute, you little bastard? (*Picks up Baby, inspects it.*) Ah-ah, I mean (*Laughs nastily.*) you little— what's the female for "bastard" eh? (*Laughs nastily, tickling baby.*)

BABY: Na-na-na- na-na-na-

NIGHT CLERK: I'll fix you, you little twirp— (*Drops Baby back in carriage, wags finger at it.*) You— you just can't come dropping in here like there's a little place all reserved for you around here, because there isn't! Understand? (*Turns and pounds register with fist.*) And there's one or two little questions we want answered right here and now, before you get any further, understand? Like who in the hell sent you rolling in here and where exactly—

BABY: Da-da— Da-da—

NIGHT CLERK: And if the Establishment doesn't get the proper answers, from somebody somewhere, there's going to be plenty trouble, get me? Let me tell you, you little— when

I was in the Army, you answered the questions that were put to you, or else!

BABY: Da-da-da— Da-da-da-

NIGHT CLERK: (*circling the carriage*) Bah-bah, bah-bah, bah-bah! You little— blithering— (*Snatches up Baby.*) idiot! Blah, blah, Mazda, Mazda, Mazda! You little incomprehensible unknown blithering— (*Sputters, shaking Baby.*) transient! (*Drops Baby back in carriage, runs hand through hair, shouting.*) Gad! I can't stand— I'm losing my— I can't stand it a second longer, I'm— It wouldn't be so bad if— somebody would wire ahead or something or— give us a little advance notice or something or— a little—

BABY: Na-da— na-da—

NIGHT CLERK: What are we supposed to do, read the birth notices in the paper every day to know who's coming, who to expect and—

BABY: Na-da- Na-da—

NIGHT CLERK: It's just too much! Like that bunch of railway signalmen arrived one night unannounced— a convention or a strike or something— and wanted to know how to get this and that, find this and that, how to get from here to someplace else, and on and on and on! You'd think at least railroad signalmen at least would know where in hell they're going and who's directing traffic and who's at the controls and all that, fer Christ's sake, now wouldn't you? (*Picks up Baby, shakes it again.*) Wouldn't you!

BABY: Nananananananana!

NIGHT CLERK: All right, all right, all right! (*Turns and shakes fist at feet passing at windows, then at audience.*) All of you! With your blind feet! Taking you who knows where! Like as if any of you even knew what brung you in here! Incomprehensible transients! Inscrutable wanderers! Victims of amnesia!

BABY: Nada— Nada— Nada!

NIGHT CLERK: (*Runs to windows and throws one open.*) All of you! Hear me? Back and forth, forever and ever and ever, is that it? Where to and where from! Well, who cares? Get me? Who gives a— I don't care, let me tell you— Little Maurice doesn't give a ferk what in hell you're all up to everywhere! And I'll just show you what— (*Runs to desk, bends under it, pulls up old rifle, rushes to carriage, snatches up Baby, runs to stairs left.*) I've had enough of this big con game, hear? Get somebody else to ferret things out, get somebody else to get the facts for the Register. I won't put up with it any longer, and I don't have to, either, hear? Make up your own vital statistics! Your own little reasons and rationalizations and aliases and alibis for living! I don't have to put up with any more of your eternal— dumb— (*Sputters.*) ant-like! blind! perambulations! Don't come sucking around *this* Establishment anymore, looking for someplace to flop! Try some other place on some other planet and see how far you get, without proper baggage, without— (*Sputters.*) without any— (*Calls up stairs.*) And— and all you Mazdas, all you Mazdas sneaking in each others' rooms and all that, you can damn well clear out, and I mean *now!* I'll— I'll get rid of every last one of you right here and now, clear out the place once and for all, I'll just show you who's running things around— (*Starts up stairs with Baby, waving gun.*) A little Spring house-cleaning, that's what! Something this world needs every so often, just to clear the air, clear out the riffraff! I'll throw you all out on your big fat heads! I've got the authority, and I'll just show all of you just who's who and who's Master on this little— (*Disappears up stairs, shouting.*) There's still a few of us left who know who— (*sound of great hub-bub upstairs*) Out, out! All— all of you! Drop dead! Drop— dead!

A medium-size light bulb is thrown down the stairwell and breaks on stage. Then a large bulb. Then an enormous bulb. As each bulb crashes, louder than the preceding one, the light on the stage is diminished, the last crash leaving all in darkness; no more feet pass at the windows.

Clock tolls endlessly in the darkness. Train whistles far off. In the darkness a very small light bulb is lowered very slowly and hesitantly down the stairwell. It grows brighter and brighter as the houselights come up.

MOTHERLODE

.

"that crotch was once a vision of love. . . ."

—Phillip Lamantia (*Peroxide Subway*)

A MINER and his Pack Animal

PHOTOGRAPHER

MODEL

THE SCHMUCK

LITTLE SCHMUCK

Some Birds

MOTHERLODE

SCENE ONE

*A desert reach. Yellow light. Yellow ground, rising slightly
to the left. Sound of continuous laughter, jukebox music,
and slot machines whirring and ringing, off right. Sound
begins to fade as Miner enters, right, leading a very small
Pack Animal loaded with pick, axe, shovel, pans, many
books in straps, an upright typewriter strapped on top.*

MINER: (*About fifty. Short and fat. Small, pointed beard, hearing
aid in one ear, with wire to pocket.*) "Don't leave!" some
one says. "Leave where?" I answer! (*Tugs at Pack Animal.*)
Come on! Where did I pick you up, anyway? Some party or
other I picked you up at— (*Animal moves a pace or two.*)
There now— getting someplace! That's it, neither uphill
nor downhill, the straight stretch, that's it— eh, what?
(*Turns and surveys desert ahead, shading eyes.*) Hmm—
What's this place? Neither uphill nor downhill— steady,
that's it. If I could ever get off this here peninsula— Come
on! (*tugging*) Got to get going. No time to waste, after all
this time— (*Pulls head of Animal. Animal does not budge.*)
Come on, willya, Garibaldi! All my worldly goods! (*Tugs
some more, gives up, scratches head, peers off right where*

sound of laughter still is heard, looks back at Animal, takes its head, looks it in the eye, bends down suddenly, inspects Animal all over underneath, raises tail, inspects under it from all angles.) Well, well, well. Such arrangements! Never really noticed— never really stopped to— no, indeed— very interesting— fore and aft— one never really notices— (*still inspecting*) Really a marvelous invention— Feet first, hind after— hardy perennial— and all that— very interesting— indeed— a little on the cute side— but— functional— practical— efficient— helpful— healthful— useful— versatile— three-in-one and all that— yes, hmmm, well— the Greeks had a— (*Straightens up.*) Indeed, who would've ever imagined— (*Takes up halter again.*) Come on, come on!

(*Enter Photographer, left, carrying Cardboard Nude. Sets up Nude, far left, proceeds to focus on it as Miner continues to urge Animal.*)

MINER: Garibaldi! You ass! Didn't you hear me? Which language do you speak, anyway? No spikka da English? Spikka da— (*Goes round to rear of Animal, pushes it, raises foot to push it, sees Photographer and Cardboard Nude.*) Hey! You— (*Photographer turns, sees Miner, runs off as Nude falls flat. Miner rubs eye.*) Must be— (*Turns up hearing aid.*) seeing things! Did I or didn't I— (*Looks all around.*) Thought I— Well— (*Pushes Animal with foot, bends down, tries to move hind foot of Animal, can't lift it.*) What the— like being stuck on flypaper— long, long brown, sticky road and all that. (*Continues to try to move feet of Animal, one after the other.*) Stuck, all stuck— every one— everyone! Curious country, I must say. Still, I'm glad to get away— from it all— from "all that"— (*Peers back, off right, where laughter still is heard.*) All that! (*Animal moves a pace forward.*) Bravo!

Congratulations! (*Rushes around to front of Animal and shakes its front paw.*) Thata boy! Keep up the great work! Work, work, work, we gotta work! Work's what makes the world go—

(*As Miner continues, Photographer enters, left, sets up Cardboard Nude as before, prepares to photograph it, but each time he gets set, it falls over.*)

MINER: That's it— come on now, one more little step with the right foot, that's it— (*reaching for each foot, in turn*) now the rear left, now the front right, now the rear right, now the front left, now the rear left, now the— (*Straightens up, huffing.*) Whew, what a strange way to walk. Glad I don't have— (*Animal has not moved. Miner takes its head in his hands and looks it in the eye.*) Can't decide which foot first, is that it? Well I can't blame— (*Goes around to rear, raises foot, and shoves Animal. It moves a pace.*) Hooray! Now we're getting somewhere again, now we're making progress. (*Raises foot to shove again, sees Photographer.*) Well, look at that there now, another bloomin' desert mirage, only maybe this time it's real. The real thing this time, I do believe— (*Turns up hearing aid, waves hat at Photographer who does not see or hear him.*) Hey you! You there, yoohoo there! I say— where you hail from, stranger? Never seen no one like you two in these parts before. I say— I come from the Salto district, pardner— hear me? My old man was the horse tamer there. Know him? Or meat packer— same damn thing. Hear me? (*Photographer neither sees nor hears. Miner tugs at Animal, drops halter, starts off alone toward Photographer, stops, returns, tugs at Animal, drops halter, starts off again alone, stops, returns. Same business over and over during following monologue.*) Hey— my friend— like I was saying— my old man was a Salto, get

it? Settled the region— manner of speaking— descended
from thirty-three gauchos— manner of speaking— whole
town descended, hear me, from thirty-three gauchos. Yeah.
All same name, most likely— Salto, or Sorel, or Laurel,
or Laureles, or Coyote, or Keyote, or whatever. All the
same and all different. One big happy— one little happy—
one—

(*As Miner continues, Photographer sets up Cardboard Nude
so that it stays up, backs off on tiptoe, rushes off stage left,
returns instantly with portable toilet, squats on it, relaxes.
Beatific expression.*)

MINER: One big sad happy little tragic— Say, just what in hell is
(*Fusses with hearing aid.*) going on over there, anyway?
(*Shades eyes to see, straining forward, tugging at Animal.*)
I see, I see! Hmm, yes, indeed, I see. That's progress, yes
indeed, that is an advance, indeed, really getting somewhere
in this world, what I mean, we're getting somewhere, after
all— everything, everything portable these days— Carry
your own everything, that's right, your own portable woman
or whatever, yes, indeed, listen to the World Series at the
Opera, if you want to— anything— and— and to think I
thought we were just standing still, not getting anywhere.
My, what a relief. (*Sighs as Photographer relaxes on toilet.*)
Tuned to his favorite station! I wonder if— uh-oh— There
she goes again. (*Nude falls over.*) Feet of clay! They're all
the same, all the same— though I keep hoping— (*Shouts
across at Photographer as over a great divide.*) Don't get
discouraged pardner! Stick to it. I'm with ya! Keep going,
no matter what, rain or shine— The flush toilet wasn't built
in a day, you know. Greatest invention since the wheel, of
course. Great leap forward and all that— (*Photographer
resumes setting up Nude, which continues to fall over.*)

Listen, Mister. As I was telling you— maybe you could
give me some line on— You seem quite advanced, all things
considered. That is, uh— do you think it's at all possible
to find the ideal— the ideal society? Some place or other
with nothing bugging anybody— no manias or anything—
except maybe a mania to kiss all the time? A *real* land of
lovers, maybe? Their country made of large white sheets?
I mean— as I was telling you— I've prospected all over
this here peninsula, hear me? Never got this far North before— "Up" is "North" isn't it? You know— all me life
I been prospecting, all over, always on the go, on the make,
you might say, yeah— (*short laugh*) That's it— ear to the
ground, eye on the future, nose to the grind— What? (*Gets
down and tries to move Animal's feet forward, one at a
time.*) That's right— like as if there was always something
I couldn't find enough of where I already was. You'd think
I'd've been happy *somewhere,* now wouldn't you? People
who laugh a lot are really happy, aren't they, everybody
knows that. (*Straightens up, peers at Photographer again.*)
Yeah— Now wouldn't you? (*Photographer bursts out
laughing as he works with Nude, laughing louder and louder
each time Nude falls over.*) Fool's gold! Is that it, Mister?
Who can tell? Well, they tell me if I ever get off this here
peninsula, if I can ever reach the mainland, I'll really strike
it. Like I'm crawling up a lady's leg or something! Speaking
of peninsulas! (*Laughs unroariously.*) Pot of gold up there!
Yeah— Mother's loaded! Undreamed riches! What? Listen,
Mister, you think I'm crazy, is that it? Not worth noticing,
huh? Well, let me just show you a thing or so. If you'll just
step over here for a momento, I'll show you who's crazy.
You see these here veins in the ground? I'm following these
here veins, see, in case you think I'm just some nut or something. I'm not one of these fly-by-night imbecile Sunday as-
sayers or fortune hunters, no sir. These veins mean business,

hear me? All leading somewhere central, see? The thing is to know if they're leading "away from" or "to" the big thing, see? I don't mind telling you. You can't steal my secrets, no sir. This here little blue vein branching and branching, this tiny little blue varicose vein, so delicate, so hard to follow sometimes, which you wouldn't think was anything particular at all— Well— (*Fiddles with hearing aid.*) Got to get going. Wasted enough time. (*Pulls pick out of pack on Animal.*) Yes, sir! Got to turn to, now. Not getting any younger and all that. (*Commences to dig shallow trench in direction of Photographer.*) The real thing isn't for the asking, my slick friend. No indeedee. It takes real work to draw blood in this life, my friend, let me tell you, if you want to get the goods out of this earth, you've really got to dig, my friend, not just scratch the silver service, let me tell you. (*Photographer has gotten Nude set up again, goes behind it, squats on toilet, relaxes. Dreamy expression.*) If you really want to find the real, pure, unadulterated thing itself, my friend— (*digging, head down*) You've got to give up everything else and— (*breathing hard*) One doesn't— just— sit around dreaming— until the real thing— comes along. Hear? (*Photographer flushes toilet, runs off with it, left, as Nude falls flat.*) Hey— hey, Mister! (*Fiddles with hearing aid.*) For God's sake, what— You were just about to— (*Strains to see, fiddles with hearing aid, shakes head.*) Was I seeing— seems like I— (*Begins to dig again, very slowly. Some yellow birds flit about, far left, very silently.*)

A desert waste. Sparse, furze-like underbrush, rather like light down on a woman's leg. Yellow light, not as bright as before. Reddish yellow ground, rising to the left. Miner, now considerably older, is digging uphill in trench which is now four feet deep. The Pack Animal is no longer to be seen.

MINER: Neither uphill nor downhill. "Keep straight on" they always said. "You cawn't miss it, old chap." Etcetera, etcetera— (*Straightens up.*) Still— seems like a slight upward— (*Digs again.*) Seems like I never git down deep enough, exactly— really underground— (*Stops again.*) Seems like I'm climbing all the time, somehow, instead of getting deeper and deeper. (*Digs again.*) Still— it's obvious I'm getting somewhere, after all— neither uphill nor— (*out of breath*) downhill— but still getting somewhere, eh? (*Straightens up again, huffing.*) Just as if— (*Shades eyes, surveys in all directions.*) Yeah, I sure prospected all over this here landscape— all up and down— like the palm of my— Still it looks different around here, sort of— (*Chuckles.*) It always looks "different" don't it? (*Digs again.*) Like they say, if you could only reach the mainland I used to hear tell of. Got to keep going, anyway, no matter what, eh? (*Straightens up again, shading eyes.*) And in the right direction. That's what counts. Not so easy eh? What

with all these little offshoots running all over. (*Digs again.*)
Branching and branch-off, every whichways. Like you never
know what you got. Hey now, what's— (*Drops pick, bends
down out of sight in trench.*) By Jimminy, this proves—
(*Raises human skull, full of dirt.*) Salud, oldtimer! (*shaking
dirt out of skull*) Well, well— things didn't "pan out" so
good for you, eh? And here I thought I was the first in these
here parts! (*poking dirt out of eye sockets*) Had a fine eye—
for dirt— didn't you, old dirt farmer? (*Looks skull in eye.*)
So— beat me to it, eh? Staked out your claim way ahead
of me, eh, oldtimer? (*Chuckles, fits fingers in eye sockets of
skull, grasps it like a bowling ball.*) Lost your head in the
bargain, eh? Yeah— well— (*swinging skull like a bowling
ball at shallower end of trench, right*) Like you dig over
here and I'll dig over there, daddy! OK? (*Sends skull
bowling down trench, off right.*) Strike! By Jimminy! Set
'em up in the other alley! (*Laughs uproariously.*)

(*Meanwhile, Photographer has entered, left, leading a beautiful live Model by the hand, setting up camera on tripod as
Model proceeds to pose.*)

MINER: Yeah! Well, now, pardner— Dig, dig! OK? See you later,
OK? (*Chuckles.*) Your pardner's gotta— (*Picks up pick,
moves to deep end of trench again, left, swinging pick.*)
Damn, this here pick's almost shot— head loose— plum
wore out. (*Inspects head of pick.*) Damn that beast! Ran
off with the whole caboodle— all me tools and books and
papers, a lifetime of— (*Digs again.*) All I got is this to dig
with— (*Straightens up.*) Strange ground around here, in
this here painted desert— (*Takes off hat, fans face, replaces hat.*) Reddish almost, or pink, like some kind of—
flesh, almost. Cactus smell, like flesh too, sort of— Like I'm
digging in a pink wrinkle on some kind of great big body of

some sort all this time! Wow— Hey! (*Sights Photographer
and Model.*) Speaking of bodies! Man, look at that. Am I
seeing things again? Ain't that a— (*Turns up hearing aid.*)
sight for sore— like I ain't seen a live— a real live one
of those in a helluva long— (*Photographer has been adjusting his camera, adding longer and longer lenses.*) Say,
Mister, what in hell you need all those for? Can't you see
what you got, man? (*Starts to climb out of trench, slips and
falls back. Photographer keeps putting on longer lenses.*)
What the hell! You trying to get closer or farther away,
Mister? (*Shouts.*) Hey, Lady, let ME take your picture,
will you? May I offer you— (*Takes off hat in a sweeping
bow.*) the conveniences— (*Indicates trench.*) of my establishment! (*Collapses in trench, laughing, but immediately
re-emerges, serious.*) Ah, yes, yes, indeed. Let's be serious.
Take careful aim, that's right— (*Photographer has now put
on a foot-long lens and crouches under black cloth behind
camera.*) Thaaat's it. Of course. Everyone's got his own
approach, of course— (*suddenly nostalgic, hand in chin*)
Ah, yes— if only I'd taken advantage of— (*Photographer
runs to Model, removes some of her clothes, runs back to
camera, looks through it, runs back to Model, removes
more clothes, runs back to camera, looks through it, runs
back to model, removes more clothes, runs back to camera,
looks through it.*) Yes, indeed, indeed. This certainly takes
me back. I've sure seen a few sights in my day. If only I
had— well— one of these days I'll really strike it— rich—
yeah— and then— (*Photographer tries to remove more
clothes from Model but she, down to her leotards, resists.
The Photographer caresses her legs, trying to remove the
leotards.*) Ah, yes— (*Miner leans on edge of trench, hand
in chin.*) Ah, the nude leg of love! That's it, that's it—
(*Model resists violently.*) Hey— what's the hitch? Uh-oh,
women don't like that there approach, Mister. Got to be a

little more— how shall I put it— delicate— you might
say. Hey— hey, Lady— (*Sweeps hat off with a bow.*) If
you would allow me to demonstrate the proper approach to
such matters— (*Photographer retreats to camera, puts
head under cloth.*) Mister, if you would allow me to—
Ladies don't like to take off their pretty little stockings in
broad daylight. Even in this here heat— (*Mops face with
bandanna, fans face with hat.*) Varicose veins and all that,
you know. "Veins of truth" the Spaniards used to call them.
(*short laugh*) Yeah, well— (*Photographer has brought
forth still longer lens and fitted it to camera.*) Think that'll
solve all your problems, eh? You— you schmuck! (*Laughs
uproariously.*) That's what you are, by jingo! I've hit on it
at last! Knew you reminded me of somebody. Something
about you. Fellow in highschool we used to call "The
Schmuck." (*big laugh*) Your ole man maybe! Yeah, a real
character— used to beat up on me, just for the hell of it.
Just for the hell of it! (*Laughs bitterly.*) Yeah. Voted Most
Likely to Succeed and all that. Yeah. It was always "Guess
what the Schmuck's up to now!" or "Guess what the
Schmuck pulled last night!" The Schmuck this and the
Schmuck that all the time! (*Fans face with hat.*) Whew,
it's— it's hot. (*Waves hat at Model.*) Hey, Lady. Let me
enlighten you as to your— uh— companion, so-called. You
think I'm some sort of creep or something eh? (*short laugh
and bow*) I am no Prince Charming— heh-heh— nor was
meant to be— (*short laugh*) But let me point out the real
schmuck around here, lady. It's that— that— walking—
telescopic— dingdong— (*sound of a car approaching in
the distance, off right*) that slick little fellow you got there,
lady. What the hell's he doing under that there cloth all this
time, anyway? Thinks he's at a peep show or something!
(*sound of motor approaching, much louder*) Give him a
wiggle or two, why don't you? Keep things in focus! Yeah.

(*screech of brakes, then car door slamming just out of sight, right*)

LOUD VOICE: You're certain this is the location, way out here?

2ND LOUD VOICE: Reckon it is.

1ST LOUD VOICE: Well, what's the charge?

2ND LOUD VOICE: Reckon that'll be six bucks from the outskirts.

1ST LOUD VOICE: What!

2ND LOUD VOICE: I said reckon that'll be six—

1ST LOUD VOICE: Well, there you are young man!

2ND LOUD VOICE: (*disgusted*) Gee, thanks! Big deal! (*screech of brakes, sound of car going off*)

MINER: Listen, lady— do you hear me or don't you? (*Fiddles with hearing aid.*) I keep this thing turned off most of the time— (*Chuckles.*) Turn the world off anytime I feel like it— you hear me OK?

(*Enter The Schmuck, right, chewing gum and swaggering slightly. Same age as miner. Portly. Thin lips, small eyes. A sharp dresser. Snapbrim hat. Canvas folding chair under arm. Topcoat over arm. Large wristwatch. Large college ring, right hand. Sunglasses. Cigar. Transistor radio in carrying case, turned on. Camera in carrying case slung from shoulder. Very small portable TV under arm. Financial newspaper in one coat pocket, large picture magazine rolled in one hand. Sees Miner and stops short behind him as Miner continues shouting at Model, then suddenly kicks Miner in the back and clouts him with rolled magazine.*)

MINER: (*falling out of sight in trench*) Wha— aw— ah— ow—

SCHMUCK: (*dropping magazine and striding forward to Photographer & Model*) What's HE doing on the set, fer Christ's sakes! (*Shoves Photographer out from under cloth on camera.*) Fer Christ's sakes, dint I tell you get an isolated spot? And the first thing I run on is some kibitzer! Where

the fuck he come from? (*handing Photographer money*)
Now would you just please— just— (*Motions him off.*)
I'll take over now, sonny. Just you take a break, and—
(*Photographer fades off, left.*) There now! (*Rubbing hands
together, he turns to the Model who has remained fixed in
pose.*) Well, here we are! Mmmm— yessss— Now, if you
would permit me— uh— what's your name, baby? (*Un-
folds canvas chair upon the back of which the word Pro-
ducer appears, and dumps all the paraphernalia he's carrying
on it.*) There, now, there we are, there we go, now—(*Goes
behind camera and sights through it.*) Mmmmm— yes—
there we are indeed— mmm— what did you say they called
you, baby? Stage name or what? Just—

MINER: (*rising slowly*) What in the name of Schmuck— hit me—
that time? Would you mind letting me in— on what—
exactly— (*Rubs face, shakes head, adjusts hearing aid,
peers left and sees The Schmuck.*) Well, speak of ole
Schmuck, and who shows up but big brother hisself! Yeah!
Where did HE materialize out of? (*still pulling himself together, brushing himself off, etc.*) Like they used to say at
school— "He wasn't born, he just suddenly materialized at
the corner of Hollywood and Vine." Yeah. Say, what's—
(*Picks up fallen picture magazine next to trench.*) Well,
well, good old *Death Magazine!* Big brother's very own, no
doubt— heh-heh. Yeah. (*spreading out magazine*) Same
old phoney crap! Even out here it follows me! Same old lies
and—

SCHMUCK: (*crooning to Model, simultaneously with above*) Baby,
you said it— we're going to— (*rubbing his hands together*) Let's just rearrange that pose a little now, shall we?
May I suggest a more— reclining position, hmm? If you
don't mind, we'll— (*Starts rearranging her pose, handling
her more and more intimately.*) That's more like it, now—
hmmm— yes— that's got it. Just what we had in mind,

yes. Just a little more— Ah, yes— just a minute, just a moment— (*Turns dial of his transistor radio until he gets music.*) There we are! Now— now we're ready to shoot, if—

MINER: (*shouting at Model*) Hey, Lady! Are you going to let that— that— schmuck— crawl all over you, Lady? How come you let that guy walk right up and take over, like you had a date or something, huh? Just like that, the schmuck's climbing all over you like he owned— (*Starts to climb out of trench but falls back. The Schmuck has succeeded in getting model in a fully reclining pose.*) Is that what they call the "real thing" back where you come from, Lady? (*Snorts, and sings.*) "But until the real thing comes along, I'll string along with you!" Yeah— Even out here it follows me— The whole boatload of— (*waving his pick at them*) Thought I left all that behind— got away from all that, I thought— schmuck of cities! Carrier of *Death Magazine!* Even out here on the real last frontier you catch up with us with your— your— (*The Schmuck has succeeded in removing the Model's leotards and presses himself on her.*) Go ahead schmucker! Go ahead! She's yours, all yours! (*Waves his pick wildly at them.*) A real choice piece of tail, man! Fruit of the loom! Sweet snatch! Crotch which once was a vision of love! (*He collapses on edge of trench as the light fades.*)

(*The Schmuck now lies on top of Model, grunting. She makes small, unreal, passionate cries. Mynah birds flit about in the fading light, crying "Love! Love!"*)

SCENE THREE

Another dusk. At far left, the edge of a dark, wiry wood. At right, the trench, now over five feet deep. The Miner is not visible. His pick lies beside the trench in the hair-like under-brush. Presently his head appears, hatless, dishevelled, much older looking. The head faces about, first one way, then the other. Eyes glazed, mouth hanging open. From time to time a distant drone is heard, off right.

MINER: (*voice low*) Wind gone— Birds gone— Sights down— Light gone, again— again and again— over and over— (*Faces left at end of trench.*) What's now? As if— (*Strains to see ahead.*) As if in some dream again— the old visions come back again, over and over— (*Snorts.*) Childhood dreams! (*Yellow birds flit about in the dark wood.*) Silly illusions, silly mirages. Bah! All old illusions of— (*Fiddles with hearing aid, straining to see into the wood.*) What's there now? A dark— a damp— a nub, a knot, a nest? Crotch in the wood which once was a— a nest, of sorts. (*Mops face with bandanna.*) Yeah— whew— hotter and hotter! And darker and darker. Yeah. Still on and on. Got to keep on— (*Head disappears. Hands appear, throwing dirt out of the trench.*) Got to keep going. No question of it, after a certain point— (*Head reappears, breathing hard.*) No turning back, after a certain point. Yeah— on and on and on! (*Head disappears again, hands reappear again, throwing dirt out.*) Forever and ever and ever. Man's— (*Head reappears, peers ahead into wood.*) Man's un— quenchable— re— lentless— (*Snorts.*) thirst for— (*Head disappears again, hands reappear with dirt.*) In— satiable— hunger for— (*breathing hard*) Famous phrase for it some- where— (*peering into wood*) Man's great— (*Searches ground nearby, almost at eye level, sees pick, reaches for it, pulls it down into trench with much effort.*) There. There now— (*Raises pick, swings it into bottom of trench.*) Uh- huh! Deeper and deeper— (*Swings again.*) Harder and harder— (*puffing*) Still only one way— no other way. (*Swings pick again. Head disappears, hands reappear throw- ing dirt.*) Vein still there, by Jimminy— no doubt about it. All this time, lying there, waiting, just waiting, for some- one— (*still out of breath*) All this time— just got to— (*Digs again.*) Yeah. No doubt about it. Got to— really go underground, to make it— (*short laugh*) Still— well— (*Peers ahead into wood again.*) Is we or ain't we? Is it or ain't it all a— big old dream? Big old hairy-ass dream and illusion! (*Snorts.*) Yeah— what if it's all— not really— what if we're not really— what if, what if I'm not really— (*Mynah birds flit about in the dark wood, crying "live, live" very faintly.*) What— (*Fiddles with hearing aid.*) Now if I could ever be sure, exactly, where I'm headed— (*peering into wood, fiddling with hearing aid, as birds continue to cry very faintly*) That is— yeah— if I could ever for sure, for once and for all— make out— make absolutely certain— like— (*Reaches forward from trench, grasping underbrush. Tries to pull self out, falls back, breathing hard.*) Whew— yeah— Got to— (*Reaches out again.*) Not here but there, maybe. After all— (*Grasps underbrush with both hands, tries to climb out again.*) Like I been going— underground all this time, while all the time— (*Falls back in trench*

*again, disappearing. Sound of coughing and wretching. Long
groan. Hat appears, head under it, hand adjusting it.)*
Found that at least! *(Lifts hat, inspects it. Mass of dirt falls
on head.)* Me ole— buddy! *(Brushes off hat fondly, raises
it overhead, looks upward through it.)* Stars, by Gad!
Vast— *(short laugh, still looking up through hat)* Vast—
(Peers ahead into wood, hat still raised.) Blank! Hmmm.
Still, there's— who knows what? There's still— what?
Hmm? Not here but there. Yeah. *(Tries to climb out again.)*
Got to— get to— see if— *(Falls back again.)* Damn! I'll
be a son of a— *(Birds fly over him and back to the wood,
cawing and cawing.)* Well, I'll be a— Seems like— *(Fiddles with hearing aid.)* I really been on the goddamn wrong
track— Yeah. Well— Got to see for myself! *(Swings pick
ahead of trench and catches underbrush with it.)* There
now, by Gad, I'll— *(Struggles to pull himself up and out
with pick, breathing hard.)* Not down— but up— That's it.
All these years. Not up but down— *(Still struggling to get
out, breathing harder)* Yeah— like I wasted all these—
While all the while— all the while— plain as day— out in
the open— mine for the taking— for all to see— anyone
to find— *(Birds fly over him and back to the wood, calling
and cawing.)* Plain to anyone— any numskull— with eyes
to see, ears to— *(Falls back in trench again.)* Ah, hell!
For Gad's sake. After all these years, can't even— when
the time comes— can't even get— *(Swings pick ahead
again. It fails to catch on underbrush.)* Hell! *(Disgusted,
looks down, surveying trench.)* Over and over— all a big
mistake— not up but down— all this time— Maps, drill-
ings, assays, testings, over and over— into Nowhere! Use-
less! For all intents and purposes, for any practical— See
it all now, by Jimminy— *(The distant droning is a little
louder now.)* Yessir, clear as anything, clear as the hair on
your— *(Swings pick ahead again, catching it on under-*

brush.) Yessir, yessirree, very clear, very very clear! Dug
my own— little— (*Pick comes loose, and he swings
again.*) That's it— We dig our own— (*Swings again.*) our
own little old— beds— our own— (*breathing hard, trying
to pull himself out*) One doesn't— just— sink— into the
ground— by— by gravity! No sir, no sirree— (*Breathing
very hard, gets torso out on top of ground at last.*) There,
by Gad! Made it! This time I'll— still a little life in the
old— (*In the dark wood, the birds flit about again, cawing
and crying "Love! Love!" very shrilly.*) Guess this proves—
proves I still— (*Pulls self along ground with pick, eyes on
the dark wood.*) Guess this proves once and for all, by Gad,
that— you don't— that underground ain't the only way,
by Gad— ain't the only way to get where you ain't, in this
here— claim I staked— no sir— plain enough— yeah—
like as if— whole life of— whole long life of— (*Raises face
to sky, fiddles with hearing aid as droning gets louder, beginning to sound very much like a machine gun firing.*)
Seems like I— what the— as if— after all this— (*Breathing very hard, twists his head around to look off right, then
up at sky again, hand to hearing aid as droning gets still
louder.*) By Gad! Seems like— as if— what— (*Puts ear
with hearing aid to ground, looking off right.*) By damn!
What I— what you— run away from— still runs—
(*Starts crawling forward frantically through the underbrush
which catches on his clothing and holds him back.*) Still—
runs— after— Damn— I still— I'm still— still coming—
still— now— I'll find— (*The drone, very loud now,
seems to be almost on top of him as he twists his face to the
sky again. His head suddenly falls back on the ground, face
up. The droning is prolonged almost interminably, then very
gradually becomes a slow staccato. The body makes a last
convulsive movement and the mouth drops open as the
drone becomes a slow rattle. Little Schmuck, a child no*

more than four feet tall but dressed exactly like The Schmuck,
chewing gum and acting exactly like The Schmuck, slowly
swaggers in, right, idly whirling a child's rattle on a stick,
wanders up to Miner, looks down at him, still twirling his
rattle absently, stops still, moves Miner's face with his foot,
turns the rattle again very slowly, still looking down at face
and chewing gum. The birds, nested now in crotch of wood,
lisp "Love, love!" very distantly, like an echo of themselves.)

THE CUSTOMS COLLECTOR IN BAGGY PANTS

THE CUSTOMS COLLECTOR IN BAGGY PANTS

The scene, a ladies' washroom on an ocean liner. He addresses the ladies in the pay toilets.

CUSTOMS COLLECTOR: Pardon me, ladies, forgive me for interrupting you at your devotions, but there is an urgent matter at hand, a pressing problem which will not wait, a certain famous diamond has been lost or stolen, and we have received cables containing certain information which led us to believe that this very diamond may very well be found upon persons of the female sex aboard this vessel, and so therefore this has necessitated my search of these private premises of you ladies, since before anyone can be allowed ashore the diamond must be found and returned to its rightful owner, and I may tell you parenthetically that we know the owner to be a hearty male of sound mind and limb, which makes the loss all the more distressing, since it is not just nobody who has lost his treasure, it is indeed a fine upstanding specimen such as myself who has lost it, and (*A tittering is heard among the ladies.*)

therefore, ladies, I find it an unavoidable duty at this time to institute a thorough search of yourselves as required by the regulations governing the conduct of existence in this lifeboat full of flush-toilets which we call civilization, and since we are about to make port if only we can find the right pilot and the right channel, I must therefore institute

my search and seizure at once, if you will allow me, because as the Customs Collector I must perforce collect all
duties on said diamond, as well as collecting the diamond
itself, as well as retrieving the treasure itself from wherever
it lies buried, if indeed it does lie, which is itself a point to
be questioned, since this strange and wonderful diamond of
hope is one which seems to be able to rise up of its own
accord and then bury itself in some generally inaccessible
place from which it never wants to be extricated, and so
lies low between the crowings of the cock until such a time
as it takes it into its head to rise again, and its disconsolate
and insensate owner is awakened in dead of night to find
his treasure risen again and buried again in some strange
place where it is harder to find than a snake lost on ship-
board, and I am no nasty old man but really still a young
buck in the prime of life, and yet it sometimes comes to pass
that in the very prime we are, so to speak, cut short, and
where we once had a fine old home-wrecker of the greatest
sensitivity, an instrument suited for large women and small
cows, a real woman's home companion, that is, why then
suddenly, I say, we find ourselves one day reduced to only
a waterspout, and a lazy one at that who just won't get up
any more, and its disconsolate owner, to whom I have pre-
viously. referred, can only bemoan and bewail the loss of
that fine upstanding diamond-head needle and divining rod,
and so my dear ladies, if you will allow me, if you will just
give me some sign or signal transmitting to me your per-
sonal permission for me to proceed with my search through
this floating world in which we are all hung-up in the search
for that lost thing upon which the customs must still be
(*A laughing is heard among the ladies.*)
continually collected nevertheless, no matter where or in
what condition it now lies and will not rise up and show
itself but may still lie hidden for days at a time and yet still
arise on the seventh day and stand again at the right hand,

ah yes, he will arise again, believe me ladies, if you will just be patient I will unearth for you that great hidden treasure again, and if I now detect a certain sniggering and moaning in your midst, as if you were thinking that I have lost my marbles, I want you to know that my marbles are one thing which I have not lost, and in fact I have them right here, right here at hand, so to speak, and they are themselves gems of the very greatest worth, let me assure you, in case you should be beginning to doubt and deride my marbles, and I can assure you that each of them could bring you great things, and I always keep them hanging handy for just such occasions, on the ready, so to speak, yes, and I've got them here somewhere, if you will bear with me for a moment, I'm sure I had them with me, I always carry them with me wherever I go in this floating universe, in this fit of existence called life, for they are truly inseparable, these twin gems who will let nothing come between them, and yet, and yet whenever that great King of Diamonds rises up, as I have before described, whenever that great tyrant arises and goeth forth for the night then there is indeed great stress and strain created between my two little gems, but ladies I do not mean to regale you with old wives' tales as to the history of our customs, I merely mean to do my duty in the search for that lost treasure and in the collections involved therein, and therefore now I would ask you ladies one by one to allow me to investigate the problem (*A moaning is heard among the ladies.*) to its very roots, for we must do everything in our power to find again that strange lost thing, for we will all die without it, like the land that fell fallow when the Fisher King fell sick and "Balls!" cried the Queen, "If I had two I'd be king-size, what with the knockers I've already got" which is somewhat beside the point I'll admit, and yet I must investigate and overturn every clue as to the nature of our existence, if I am to discover the true hiding place of that same thing we all search, and it's a true adage that wherever there are nuts there are squirrels, and you ladies naturally are not nested here without purpose, so that I have a perfect right to suspect you may very well have that something of great importance hidden upon your very person, oh yes, for I remember well what one lady said to me once in a former investigation, she said "Is that a flashlight in your pocket, honey, or do you really love me?" and I said, I said "Lady, if that's the way you feel, you will have to come along with me, you will have to come along with the Collector, for there are internal revenues to be collected as well as the usual customs, and if you feel that way, lady, you must feel pretty good, especially from behind, if you will allow the search to continue, etcetera, etcetera" but of course, ladies, this is a slightly different case we have before us, or at least an outrageous extension of the original case of search and seizure, and so if you ladies persist in not cooperating in the slightest, if that's the way you ladies feel, why then I shall be forced to take things in my own hands, so to speak, I will have to weigh the problem carefully and see where I can lay it, that is to say, lay your fears to rest, (*A singing and a moaning is heard among the ladies.*) if you'll just be patient, I'm coming to it, I'm coming to your most pressing problem, I'm coming to lay your problem, so don't be embarrassed by my contortions and probings and reachings, I'm merely trying to get hold of the problem, I'm trying to nail down the problem, I'm trying to lay that ghost once and for all, if you will allow me, if you will excuse me for calling that diamond-head rattler a ghost, and yet He is in fact exactly like a ghost who refuses to stay in a lying-down position all the time, for this here Ghost of Love, this very totem-pole of love always rises up again, by god, and "Thar she blows!" cries Ahab afloat upon his Moby Dick, but now, now for some reason, ladies, as I told you before, something has happened to that mobile dick of a sea-serpent so that he riseth not to the bait anymore, and so now I'm afeard and afraid, I'm sore afraid that someone has bit off that fine free leg of mine since I cannot for the wife of me find it anywhere anymore though I search high and low and fear more and more to hear that flushing out of the old and the flushing in of the new which is the fate of every generation, ah yes, and it's a race to see what or who'll go down the drain first, and I am deathly afraid I am indeed approaching that great sieve of existence through which we must all pass, and me without a paddle, me without an oar, me without my gun, me without my mobile which no longer swings, for my little diamond-snake has slipped his noose somehow, or one of you has stolen it, yes, that's it, to get to the point of all this, it's becoming more and more evident to me as my investigation reaches its climax that you very ladies have pulled a fast one and given us the slip, you women have stolen our most precious stones, yes, fair ladies, graces, mothers and charmers, I see you all clearly now in your separate cages like so many tellers in pawnshops where I temporarily hocked myself, and I have the sudden feeling that I have seen you all before, have indeed known you all personally before, and here are assembled all the women I have ever loved or known, and I see you all now *(A singing and a moaning among the ladies grows louder, almost like the sound of water lapping.)*

stretched out before me as one great body in which I hid myself, just as now you have finally hidden in you that most valuable codpiece of my life, yes, it has somehow gotten swallowed up in you, and I am nowhere and nothing without it, oh let me find that thing again, recapture it once more, let me catch the one of you who has taken it, come on now, let me in there, out with it before I shoot, and never mind all that moaning and groaning and protesting, and be very careful what you do with it for it is loaded and will go off easily, yes, I'm warning you that you're dealing

with a hardened criminal who is desperate and will shoot almost at sight, I'm warning you to be sure to have it pointed away from you at all times or else the Management cannot be responsible for what might materialize, and in fact let me give you a helping hand in this matter, I beg you let me help you get it into the recommended safe position, for it is liable to go off half-cocked, and so, and so if that gypsy winch among you who has hauled in my hauser will now please raise your right hand or other appendage so that I may come to your aid, so that I may indemnify you, so that I may rectify, so that I may be rejoined to that lifetime ally of mine, my own blood and bone, my own power and glory and no one else's, without which I am as good as dead, for I will never be satisfied with anyone else's and will gladly undergo any kind of treatment in order to retrieve my roamin' candle, my very warhead, my ship's head, my death's head, yes, for I would truly die without it, and I assure you it will do *you* no good whatever in the end unless I am reunited with it first, so that if you will now allow us to be reunited I will in short be able to reward you most handsomely in person, but, but it seems by your cries and tragic lamentations that you cannot in any way bear to part with my most dutiable Hope Diamond and would in fact yourself die without it, in which case I can only beseech you to have mercy on those two orphans which have been left behind and without a father, those two matching marbles which earlier I had some trouble in locating, those two little ones which I have now refound abandoned in my hanging gardens, those poor twins who ache to be reunited with their master, and so, and therefore, my fine lady, you whom I now hear making most passionate
(*The sound of many sweet voices muffled is dominated by one pure lyric voice.*)
sounds, you of the fair hair and longing voice, sweet heart's ease and heart's desire, let us come together now at last, in

most close and perfect coupling, yes, now, let me now come unto you as in the first night, sweet one, you who has my gem, my joy, my lost snake of life— (*sounds of one toilet flushing*) Oh— oh— not— not that! (*He clutches his groin in great pain.*) Oh— oh— there it— there it— (*gasping for breath*) Oh oh no— anything— anything but that! If— if I— if we— lose that— then— then what about— then what would— what else— would we— (*staggering*) Oh— ah— Feel like I— it's— it's (*sound of second toilet flushing*) It's— oh I— can't— I won't— No— you can't— You— You— (*Beats violently on doors of pay toilets.*) Stop, stop! Hear me? You in there! I— I said Stop! This can't go on! I'm— I— absolutely— refuse to— (*sound of many toilets flushing. It blends with the sound of many voices murmuring and crying like the sea itself.*) Hear me! Whoever— whatever you are— in there! All of you! You— you can't do this to me— to us! You can't— get away with it! (*Flushing becomes a great roar. He shouts louder and louder to be heard above it.*) Help! Help! Down the drain! Into the ocean! Lost at sea! Lost in— (*Sound of a great storm at sea, engulfing the ship. He staggers about wildly, holding his groin, shouting at the pay toilets.*) Go on! Go on! Go ahead and sink us! Sink us all! Go right— ahead! But— but— (*shaking his fists violently at the pay toilets*) But I won't drown! Not I! I won't drown, I won't go down! Hear me? I— I'll— I— I won't *die*. I won't capitulate! I absolutely refuse to die! (*Sudden and complete darkness. The storm continues.*)